SCIENCE & MATH
ENRICHMENT ACTIVITIES
FOR
THE PRIMARY GRADES

Elizabeth Crosby Stull, Ph.D.
Carol Lewis Price, M.A.

The Center for Applied Research in Education, Inc.
West Nyack, N.Y.

Library of Congress Cataloging-in-Publication Data

Stull, Elizabeth Crosby.
   Science & math enrichment activities for the
primary grades.

   Includes index.
   1. Science—Study and teaching (Primary)
2. Arithmetic—Study and teaching (Primary)
3. Activity programs in education—Handbooks, manuals,
etc. I. Price, Carol Lewis. II. Title.
LB1532.S76   1986   372.3'5044   86-8322

ISBN 0-87628-746-1

PRINTED IN THE UNITED STATES OF AMERICA

CONTENTS

Section 8
MICE AND FRIENDS 117

Background Ideas and Other Helpful Things to Know • 117

Activity Suggestions • 117

Reproducible Activity Pages • 122

Section 9
UP, UP, AND AWAY! 135

Background Ideas and Other Helpful Things to Know • 135

Activity Suggestions • 136

Reproducible Activity Pages • 138

Section 10
SEA LIFE **150**

Background Ideas and Other Helpful Things to Know • 150

Activity Suggestions • 151

Reproducible Activity Pages • 157

Section 11
BURSTING WITH SEEDS 170

Background Ideas and Other Helpful Things to Know • 170

Activity Suggestions • 171

Perennials and Annuals *(171)*

What's Inside a Seed? *(171)*

Estimation of Sunflower Seeds *(171)*

Compare Yourself to a Giant Beanstalk *(172)*

Seed Classification in a Muffin Tin *(172)*

Vocabulary Books *(172)*

Seeds Are Stored Food *(172)*

Plants Absorb Water *(173)*

State Flowers *(173)*

Plant an Herb Garden *(174)*

Musical Instruments *(174)*

Traveling Seeds in a Bag *(174)*

The Medicine Man and the Space-Age Medicine Person *(175)*

Reproducible Activity Pages • 176

Section 12
EACH TOOL IS SPECIAL 190

Background Ideas and Other Helpful Things to Know • 190

Activity Suggestions • 190

Tools of the Trades *(190)*

Plant and Animal Tools *(191)*

Collage *(191)*

Tool Stations *(191)*

Unusual Tools *(191)*

Homemade Tools *(191)*

Homemade Toy *(192)*

Machine Noises *(192)*

Tool Pantomime *(192)*

Tools at Home *(192)*

Categorizing Tools *(193)*

Activity Suggestions • 225

Measuring a Giant *(225)*
Two Types of Trees *(225)*
Points *(226)*
Sugar Maple Sampling *(226)*
Tree Collage *(226)*
Go on a Tree-Bark Walk *(226)*
Thanks to the Generous Trees *(226)*
Splatter Painting *(227)*

Prevent Forest Fires *(228)*
Measuring with Sticks *(228)*
Acid Rain *(228)*
Arbor Day *(229)*
A Tree and Leaf Identification Book *(229)*
A Tree-Tasting Party *(229)*

Reproducible Activity Pages • 230

14–1   The Four Seasons
14–2   Thanks to Trees
14–3   What's the Leaf?
14–4   The Sassafras Tree
14–5   Recipe for Making Paper
14–6   Taking a Closer Look at Trees
14–7   Autumn Leaves Are Falling
14–8   The Hidden Leaf
14–9   Tree Talk
14–10   Match the Leaf Shapes
14–11   An Acorn Story

Section 15
THE WAYS OF THE WIND

Background Ideas and Other Helpful Things to Know • 242

Activity Suggestions • 243

Language Experience Chart *(243)*
Colored Bubbles *(243)*
Seeds Blown by the Wind *(243)*
Making Pinwheels *(243)*

Paper Airplanes *(243)*
The Dangers of Wind *(243)*
Homemade Kites *(244)*

Reproducible Activity Pages • 245

15–1   Windy Washday Words
15–2   Up, Up, and Away in a Hot Air Balloon
15–3   High Flying Numbers
15–4   Catch the Number Word Trash
15–5   Flying Fives
15–6   Bubble Letters
15–7   Catch the Pattern
15–8   Favorite Fan Graph
15–9   Windmill Numbers
15–10   Sailing with the Wind
15–11   How Many?

Section 16
A BYTE OF TECHNOLOGY

Background Ideas and Other Helpful Things to Know • 257

Activity Suggestions • 258

Reproducible Activity Pages • 260

SKILLS INDEX

SKILL AREA	ACTIVITY SHEET NUMBER
Art	2-1, 3-10, 6-5, 10-1
Creative Thinking	1-5, 1-12, 3-9, 3-11, 4-5, 4-6, 5-2, 5-10, 6-2, 6-9, 10-5, 14-9, 16-2, 16-4
Creative Writing	1-8, 2-7, 3-4, 4-4, 5-11, 6-1, 6-7, 7-5, 8-1, 8-10, 10-7, 10-9, 10-10, 10-12, 12-5, 13-10, 14-11, 15-2, 16-6
Dramatic Expression	1-10, 2-8, 6-3, 8-6, 10-2, 11-5, 11-6
Math	
Addition	1-9, 2-9, 4-9, 6-6, 8-2, 9-2, 12-7, 13-4, 13-6, 13-8
Calendar	3-6, 5-3, 5-5
Counting	1-7, 3-8, 3-12, 4-2, 8-4, 9-1, 11-2, 11-7, 12-11, 15-5, 15-9, 15-11
Fractions	7-6, 12-8
Geometry	5-7, 5-8, 5-9
Graphing	1-3, 1-4, 7-7, 10-8, 15-8
Labeling	12-6, 16-1, 16-2
Measurement	3-5, 4-11, 8-5, 9-9
Money	7-11, 13-4
Number Words	2-3, 2-10, 4-10, 4-12, 6-8, 7-1, 7-2, 11-1, 15-1, 15-4, 16-7

SKILL AREA	ACTIVITY SHEET NUMBER

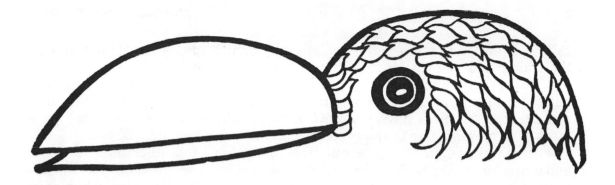

Section 1
A CLOSER LOOK AT BIRDS

Background Ideas and Other Helpful Things to Know

There are many, many birds in the world (over 8,500 species), and they vary in size, color, and shape. They also vary in the way they live (predators, scavengers, insect-eaters, seed-eaters, etc.) and in their *habitat*, or where they live (tropical forests, woods, fields, marshes, lakes, oceans).

Only birds have feathers! Feathers are made of keratin, a material like our fingernails. Feathers are useful in flight as they help to propel the bird. Also, the bright or muted colors act as a camouflage to protect the bird, and the tiny feathers layered close to the body help to keep the bird warm and dry. Feathers are extremely important and make birds unique.

Many insect-eating birds fly south (*migrate*) in winter and return in spring, often to the very same spot. Lots of energy is needed for flying, so birds are hearty eaters. The largest living bird is the ostrich and the smallest is the hummingbird.

Activity Suggestions

Migration. In late autumn, make construction paper birds with the class. Tack the birds onto a construction paper tree on the bulletin board, or staple a long piece of string onto the birds and hang them from a real tree branch that is stuck into a can of plaster of Paris. Display the birds for two to three weeks,

1

calling attention to them *daily*. Explain that many birds fly south (*migrate*) for the winter and that they may gather in flocks in a tree.

Then, one day after all children have gone home, take down the birds and put them into a labeled envelope in the bottom drawer of the desk. Next day, explain that the birds have *migrated*. Explain that scientists claim that some birds return every year to the same tree and that maybe ours will too.

In spring, begin to talk about "the first robin" and other birds that are appearing or disappearing (depending upon geographic location). Review the concept of migration. Locate the paper construction birds that are safely hidden away and make a bulletin board. Tack up the birds or hang them again on a tree branch. When children come to school the next day, they are surprised to see that the *same birds* have returned to their tree. (NOTE: Have the children print their names on the birds because some won't remember which bird was theirs.)

Help the Birds Build a Nest. Have children examine three nests. Then have them bring in all of the things that birds use to make a nest, and put them on your science table. Encourage bringing items such as string, ribbon, yarn, grasses, twigs, dried leaves, the fluff from clothes dryers, or old fiberfilled pillows. Children can construct a big nest.

Have children pound, shape, and roll plasticene (good for small muscles of the hand) into birds, bowl-shaped nests, and round eggs. Display these figures on a pile of straw at eye level or on the floor where children can use this area for creative play or to write stories.

The Flight of Birds. Using a large globe, show that birds fly *from* and *to* certain areas. Use clay, toothpicks, and colored yarn for different birds, so that children can keep coming back to the globe to check the routes. How far is it in terms of miles? Make banners showing this information. The banners can be taped to toothpicks, stuck into a little ball of plasticene, and gently pressed onto the globe next to the bird routes.

Bird Math. Have older children create story problems and have the class solve them. "If a bird flies from ____(city, state)____ to ____(city, state)____ in one day, how many miles is that?" "Where can you find the information?" (Use travel books, magazines, atlas, and auto club maps to gauge distances.)

How Long Is a Mile? Bring in a pedometer and let different students use it each day (clip it to a belt). They will begin to realize that one mile is very far.

Use a trundle wheel to measure 5,280 feet, or 1 mile. Ask: "How many times would you need to take the trundle wheel up and down the main hall? How many times around the playground?" (This is especially effective as a small group activity.)

Birdseed Sprouts. Bring in birdseed and sprinkle it on a large wet sponge, in an aluminum dish filled with water. The seed will sprout. Children are very surprised that birdseed will actually sprout! (This activity can be the beginning of a unit on seeds also.)

Daily Log. Make a large chart and label it with the days of the week. Let the children write in where the bird is and what it will see. They could also draw the information. The newspaper can be used for this activity with older students, to help bring in daily weather news and state and city news.

DAILY LOG of	
Mon.	
Tues.	
Wed.	

Bird Warm-up. Do the following exercises along with your students:

Pretend you are a bird.

Flex your shoulder muscles.

Flap your wings (arms) 20 times.

Flap your right wing 10 times.

Flap your left wing 10 times.

Turn your head to the right and look over your shoulder.

Turn your head to the left and look over your shoulder.

Bend your knees 10 times.

Jump on your right foot 15 times.

Jump on your left foot 15 times.

Fly away to a count of 10. (Flap wings and move on feet.)

Stop in the tree.

Fold in your wings (arms) slowly.

Use your fingers to grip the branch.

Slowly settle down to rest.

Bird Puppets. Make large paper-bag puppets, and have children slip them over their heads and use them for creative play. Also, get a record of bird calls from the public or school library, and have children listen carefully and try to imitate the sounds while using the bird puppets.

Bird Colors. Tie in the study of birds and color. If today is Chickadee Day, how many children are wearing yellow? How many things in the room are yellow? What else is yellow? This can be repeated with Bluejay Day, Baltimore Oriole Day (orange), Cardinal Day (red), etc.

Tie in color and bird study by planning for the next day. Designate tomorrow as Red-Headed Woodpecker Day, and wear something red or bring in something red for the "color table." (A note in advance to parents explaining that each day will be in honor of a bird/color will guarantee better results.)

Creative Writing. "Going Away versus Staying Home": Ask the children: "What news would a tree, who stayed in the schoolyard *all* winter, have to tell a bird just returning to the area? Remember, this bird is eager for *all* of the news." Try this as a total group and use an experience chart for your story, or begin as a total group to generate ideas and then have the children write their individual stories. This activity helps children with sequential thinking. Draw pictures to accompany the news. Share the stories.

Using the same technique of total group and small group activity, or a combination of the two, have a creative writing session on the topic: "What News Would the *Bird* Have to Tell the *Tree*?"

Another variation: What news would the tree and the bird have to tell the bear who is just waking up from his long winter's sleep (*hibernation*) and missed *everything*? Children could work individually and tell the bear just family news, or they could work in small groups on "Weather News," "School News," "Sports News," "TV News," "What We Learned in Math News," "What We Learned in Science News," and "What We Learned in Social Studies News." Their efforts could be compiled into folders or stapled together with a colorful construction paper cover for interesting books to add to the class library.

Conduct a Survey. Ask ten people to choose a favorite bird from your list of choices. Graph it. Make a blue ribbon for the favorite of each individual survey. Next, make the same graph on a large bulletin board or roll paper. Each student should tack up (or tape) his or her blue ribbon winner to the huge graph to determine the all-time favorite, the next favorite, the least favorite. (See Activity Sheets 1–3 and 1–4.)

Easel Painting. Share ten to twelve large pictures of very different birds from *National Geographic* or *Ranger Rick* magazines. Select birds such as the ostrich, hummingbird, swan, chicken, grosbeak, eagle, bluejay, rook, cockatoo, spoonbill, and cormorant. Emphasize the sizes, shapes, colors, feathers, beaks, and feet. Now put away the photographs and illustrations. Have a "Birds Only" sign on top of the easel, and make a sign-up sheet for students to take turns painting. Explain that this week only birds will be painted at the easel. Display the colorful paintings.

Bird Reports. As much excitement is usually generated from the study of birds, encourage students to select a bird and do a research report. By using the classroom library, school library, public library, and books or magazines from home, children can obtain factual, scientific information about birds. Be sure to have two or three sources for each report (*Natural History*, *Ranger Rick*, tapes describing birds and their calls, etc.). Record the information and report it to the class. These, too, could be compiled into a class bird book for a week or two and then returned to the students. (See Activity Sheet 1–1.)

For creative reporting, children could wear a bird hand puppet and let the bird tell all of the information about itself. Or, "Interview a Bird on TV." The person giving the report can make a colorful bird mask, or a paper bag (decorated like the bird) can be worn over the head or hand. The bird could give the interviewer a list of questions that it wants to have asked. For variation, there could be some "call-in" questions from the listening audience, to give them a chance to participate.

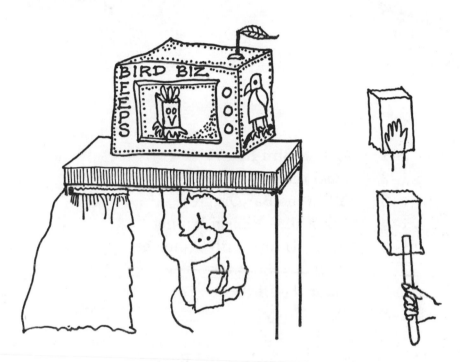

**Activity Sheets for
A CLOSER LOOK AT BIRDS**

Name _____

Date _____

WRITE A
BIRD REPORT

Use several resource books or nature magazines
from the library to complete this bird report.

The name of the bird I am reporting

on is the _____.

1. On a separate page, draw a picture of the bird in flight.

2. Bills and Beaks: A bill is usually pointed and a beak is usually curved.
   Birds use their beak, or bill, as a tool to get and handle food.

   Close-up of beak or bill   Food that this bird eats

3. Feet: Most birds have four toes, with three pointing forward and one pointing
   backward. It would make this shape footprint ⅄ . Some birds have two toes
   pointing up and two pointing down. It would make this shape footprint ✕ . Some
   birds have only three toes, and their footprints may look like this Y . Some have
   web feet.

   Close-up of bird's feet   Footprints

4. Tell some special things to know about this bird (where it lives, how it got its name, etc.).
   Write them on another sheet of paper.

Use the back of this sheet to write more interesting facts about this bird. People who study
birds are called ORNITHOLOGISTS.

Name _____

Date _____

1. Cut out the labels below of the parts of a bird.
2. Paste each label on the correct line next to the body part.
3. Color the bird.

LABEL THE BODY PARTS

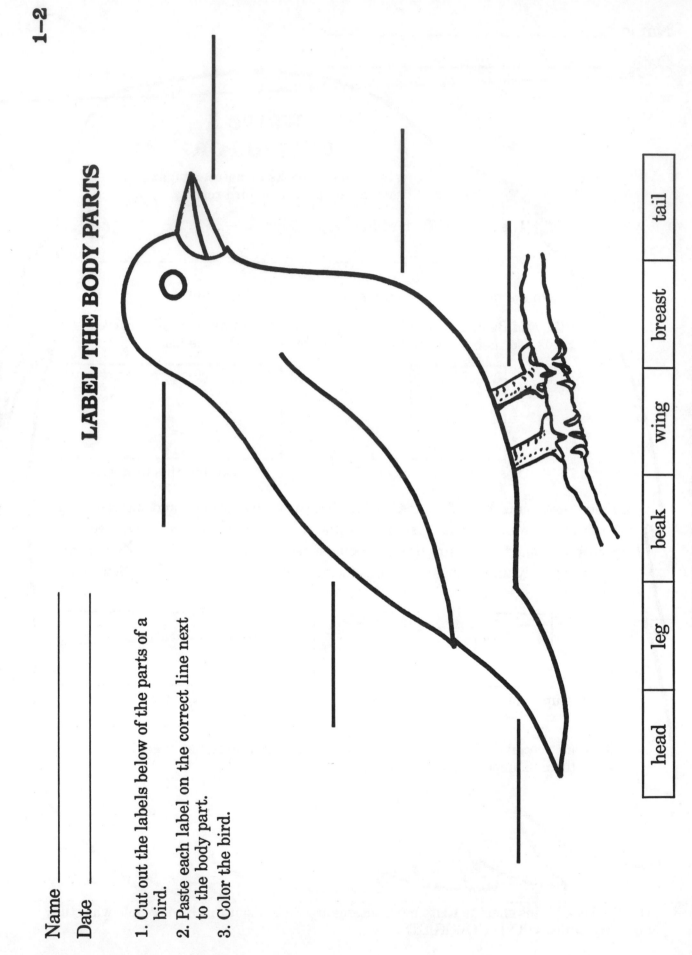

head	leg	beak	wing	breast	tail

Name _____

Date _____

FILL IN THE BAR GRAPH

1. Interview ten people, one at a time.
2. Say, "I will name five birds. Which one of these is your favorite?"
3. Color in the square above the bird selected.
4. Which bird got the most votes? Check the numerals at the left of the bar graph.
5. *Results*: Write the favorite bird's name and the number of votes on the lines here. Then draw a picture of the favorite bird on the back of this sheet.

FAVORITE BIRD _____

NUMBER OF VOTES _____

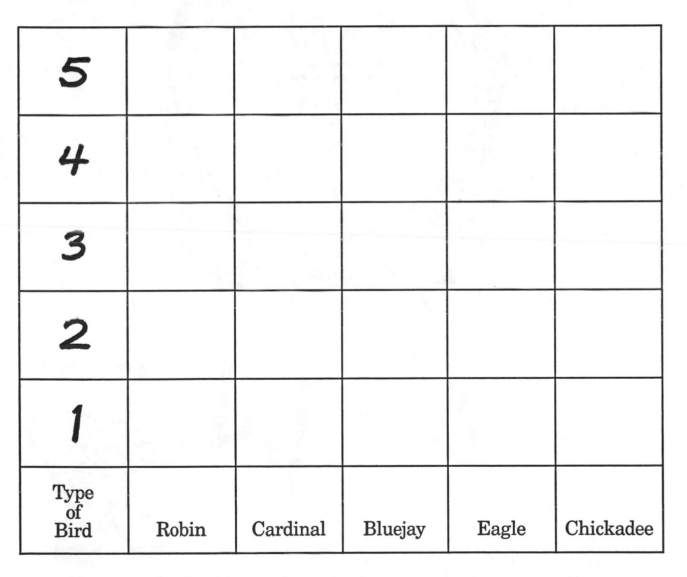

5					
4					
3					
2					
1					
Type of Bird	Robin	Cardinal	Bluejay	Eagle	Chickadee

Name _____

Date _____

PICK A BLUE RIBBON WINNER

1. Color the "Favorite Bird" below from your survey of ten people.
2. Color the ribbon blue.
3. Cut out the badge.
4. Pin the blue-ribbon badge onto the giant graph in your classroom.

Color this mini-badge and cut it out. Wear it to announce your winner.

Name _____

Date _____

CREATE THINGS WITH TRIANGLES

This cardinal's crest gives its head the shape of a triangle. What else has a triangle shape? Use your imagination and complete three pictures in the boxes below.

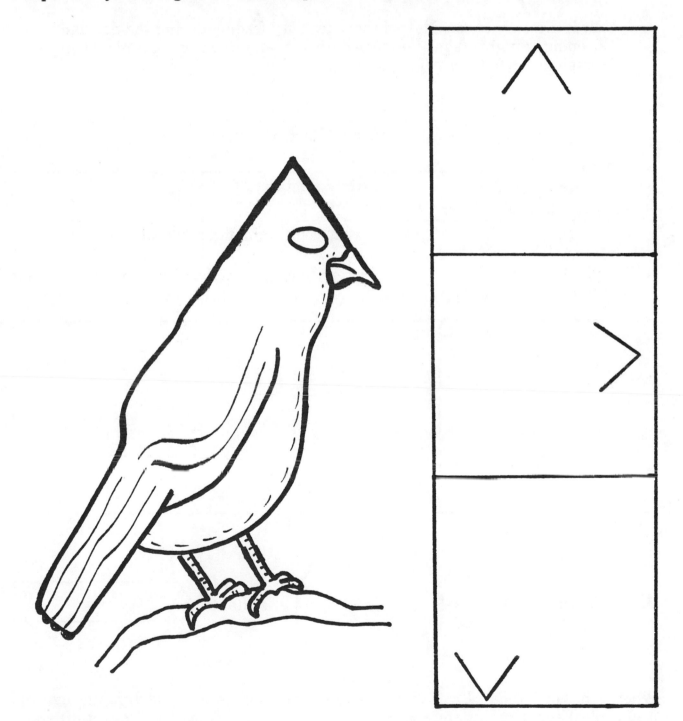

Name _____

Date _____

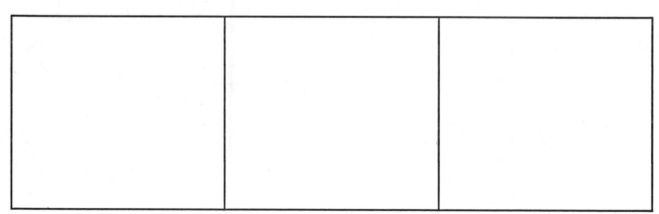

WATCH FOR THE BIRDS

Birds are easy to see. Most of them are busy feeding during the day and sleeping at night. Take some time during the day to watch for birds. Then complete the following information.

1. I saw _____.
    (name of bird or birds)

2. I heard _____.
    (bird song or call)

3. The bird colors were _____.
    (write color word and show color)

4. Draw and label three things the birds were doing. (Examples: flying, hopping, sitting on a tree limb, pulling up a worm.)

5. This is what time it was   Digital time: [   ]

When I go home today, I can turn this paper over and go bird watching in my own backyard. (Keep a record and compare it with this one.) Watch the birds at different times of the day to observe their habits. Form a Bird Watcher's Club!

Name _____

Date _____

COUNT THE BIRDS

How many birds are in each nest? Write the numeral in the square next to the nest. Now find that same numeral at the bottom of this sheet. Cut it out and paste it over your handwritten numeral.

Name _____

Date _____

DIAL A STORY

1. Cut out the three spinners at the bottom of this page.
2. Use a paper fastener to fasten one spinner to each circle. (See the sample.)
3. Spin the spinner for each circle to determine:

    Character (Who is the story about?)
    Setting (Where does the story take place?)
    Type of story (How do you plan to entertain the reader?)

4. Now write your creative story using the information the spinners point to. Remember, you can use these wheels again and again to create stories.

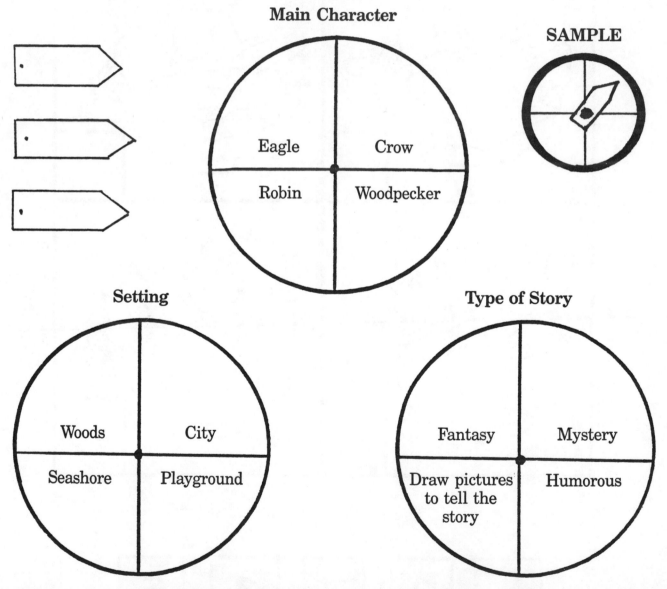

Main Character

Eagle | Crow
Robin | Woodpecker

SAMPLE

Setting

Woods | City
Seashore | Playground

Type of Story

Fantasy | Mystery
Draw pictures to tell the story | Humorous

Create your very own "Dial a Story" wheels by providing different characters, settings, and types of story.

Name _____

Date _____

ADD THE BIRDS

1. Look at one branch at a time. How many birds are on the left of the plus (+) sign? How many birds are on the right of the plus (+) sign? How many birds are there in all?

2. Find the equation at the bottom of the page that matches each branch. Cut it out and paste it next to the correct branch.

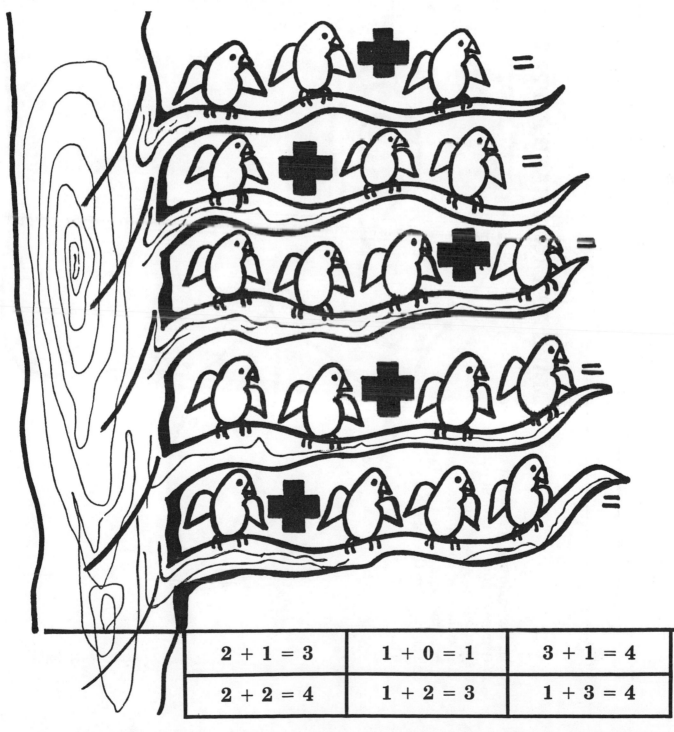

2 + 1 = 3	1 + 0 = 1	3 + 1 = 4
2 + 2 = 4	1 + 2 = 3	1 + 3 = 4

Name _____

Date _____

MAKE AN EAGLE HAND PUPPET

Color the eagle and then cut it out. Carefully trace around the cut-out pattern onto a sheet of heavy paper and cut it out. Put the two cut-out eagle pieces together. Sew around the edge with a big, blunt needle and yarn, using the dots as a guide.

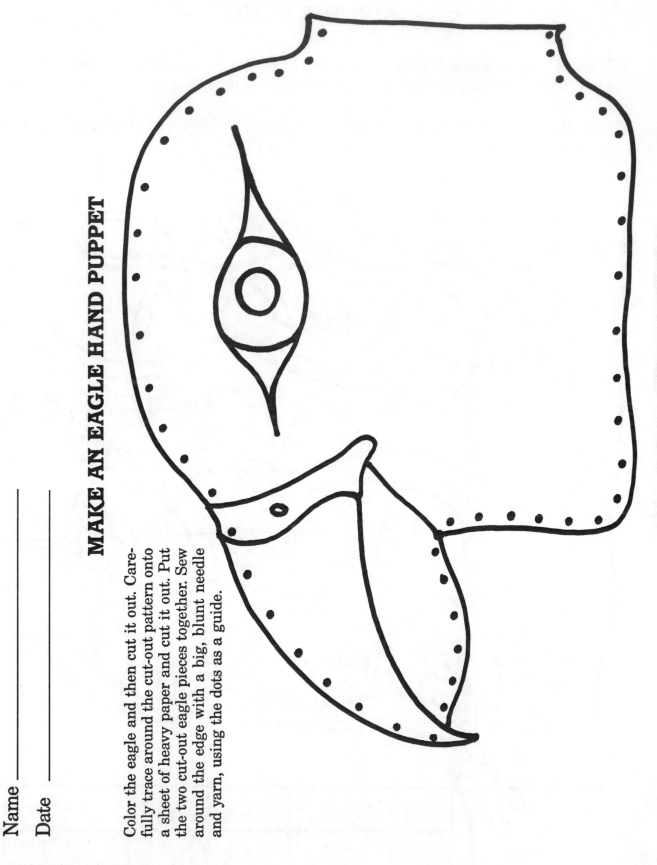

Name _____

Date _____

WISE OLD OWL MIGRATION INFORMATION STATION

In many fairy tales, the Wise Old Owl knows all of the answers to questions. Pretend that you are a young bird just setting out on your long journey. This is your chance to ask the Wise Old Owl three questions. *Think carefully!* What three things would you like to know about bird migration?

1. _____

_____

_____

2. _____

_____

_____

3. _____

_____

_____

Now, *you* can become the Wise Old Owl! Exchange papers with classmates and, on the back of this page, answer the questions. (List the source of your information.)

Name _____

Date _____

MAKE BIRDS FROM BASIC SHAPES

Do you remember the body parts of a bird? Here's your chance to make your own bird shapes. Using your crayons, draw a round bird made of just circles, using the big ◯ below for the body. Then make a square bird using just ☐ shapes. Finally, make a triangle bird using just △ shapes. Be sure to color your birds.

When finished, turn this sheet over and make a bird using the ◯ and ☐ and △. See how many of each shape you can use!

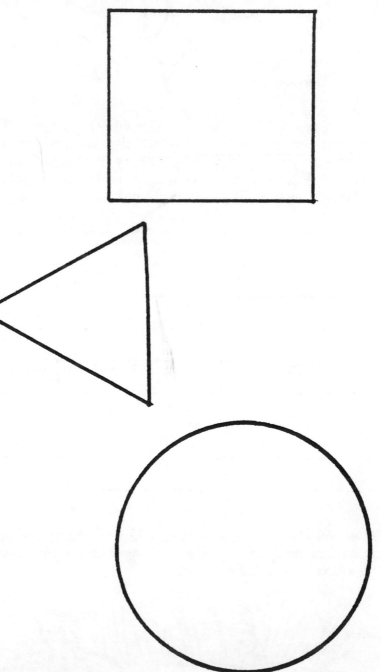

Section 2
OUR PREHISTORIC PAST

Background Ideas and Other
Helpful Things to Know

The age of dinosaurs began about 300 million years ago. For about the next 210 million years, dinosaurs dominated the earth. Many of them were the most terrifying land animals that ever lived. Huge plant-eating dinosaurs lived in swamps or along seashores. Their enemies were the meat-eating dinosaurs who threatened their lives.

The word "dinosaur" comes from the Greek words *dinos*, meaning terrible, and *sauros*, meaning lizard. Many of these creatures stood as tall as 20 feet and had skulls 4 feet long, with huge daggerlike teeth.

Some dinosaurs ate meat while others ate only plants. Usually the meat eaters walked on two legs and the plant eaters walked on four legs, but there were exceptions to this rule. The duck-billed dinosaurs walked on two legs but ate plants because they had only small teeth. All armored and horned dinosaurs were plant eaters.

Scientists learn about dinosaurs from fossils, the remains of ancient living things. Scientists who study fossils and search for dinosaur bones are called *paleontologists*. They reconstruct the skeletons of the animals so that we can imagine what these prehistoric creatures looked like, and how they may have lived.

We know about several different kinds of dinosaurs:

- The *Stegosaurus* was a plant eater, protected by armored plates down its back, with a brain the size of a walnut.
- The *Triceratops* had three horns protruding from its head and snout. It was always eating plants.
- The *Brontosaurus* was called "thunder lizard" because it was so heavy that the ground shook when it walked. It had to eat plants nearly all the time to satisfy its hunger.
- The *Tyrannosaurus Rex*, the "terrible king," was a ferocious meat eater who attacked other dinosaurs. It had powerful hind legs, while its two front legs were weak and useless.
- The *Pteranodon* was a flying reptile with wings as long as a schoolbus. This big bird had no teeth and no feathers.

No one really knows why the age of the dinosaurs ended. Some scientists believe that the earth became too cold and killed the plants that the animals needed to live. Others feel that the earth was covered with water. However, we can still "see" these huge beasts at museums throughout the world.

Activity Suggestions

Clay Dinosaurs. Give each child a lump of clay and ask the students to make a model of their favorite dinosaur. Use construction paper to create a tabletop environment, including trees, volcanoes, swamps, and bushes. Place the clay dinosaurs in the environment.

How Long Is a Brontosaurus? Measure the length of the "thunder lizard" in your hallway at school. Put tape down on the floor where you begin, measure 80 feet, and put down another piece of tape. Hang a sign in the hallway to tell others about the brontosaurus. You'll be amazed at how huge these creatures were!

Digging for Dinosaurs. Fill a plastic bucket or deep pan with sand. Hide three or four plastic dinosaurs in the sand. Have the children pretend to be paleontologists using scoops, little shovels, toothbrushes, spoons, and wire brushes.

Fossils. Talk with the students about how we have learned about dinosaurs. Although we have skeletons of the animals that show us their body structure, we don't know what kind of skin covered the bones. Wooly mammoths are the exception. Whole animals have been found frozen in the ice of the Arctic. Have the children use their imaginations to create a dinosaur. Ask: "What protective devices will your dinosaur have?" "What color or pattern will the skin be?" "What will it eat?" "Where will it live?" These pictures can be bound together to make a Prehistoric Picture Book, or a large group-made depiction can be created on butcher paper with poster paints and tacked on one wall of your classroom.

A Field Trip. Plan a trip to a local museum that has a display of dinosaurs. When you return to school, ask the children to write a story about the experience and to include drawings.

The Brontosaurus Walk. This is a creative movement activity to be read and directed by you:

WHOMP! WHOMP! WHOMP! WHOMP!

A brontosaurus walks to the swamp. (*Move heavily and slowly.*)
He bends his neck way down low,
   and eats the tender plants as they grow. (*Bend neck to floor.*)
SLURP! SLURP! SLURP! SLURP!
Ummmmm! Those plants taste very good. (*Lick lips.*)
He'd eat a lot more if only he could. (*Shake head sadly.*)
Now he turns and walks away. (*Turn and walk slowly.*)
He'll be back another day!
WHOMP! WHOMP! WHOMP! WHOMP!

Skeletons and Bones. Talk about other animal bones that children often see, such as those of chickens and turkeys from holiday dinners. Save the bones from your next chicken (or turkey) dinner. Clean them, rinse them in bleach, and dry them in the sun. Have the students see if they can arrange them on a tray in skeleton form, or identify the parts of the body from which they come. Also see if they can identify the animal or bird from which various bones come.

Meat Eaters and Plant Eaters. Have a child make a chart of meat-eating and plant-eating dinosaurs. The children can talk about the physical characteristics of each of the dinosaurs and draw pictures of each to be used on a prehistoric mural.

Meat Eaters	*Plant Eaters*
Ceratosaurus	Iguanodon
Tyrannosaurus	Triceratops
	Stegosaurus
	Brontosaurus
	Ankylosaurus
	Protoceratops
	Pteranodon

Activity Sheets for
OUR PREHISTORIC PAST

Name _____

Date _____

COLOR THE DINOSAURS

Color these two dinosaurs. Then paste them onto heavy oaktag and cut them out. Punch a hole at the top of one, string it on yarn, and use it as a necklace. Use the other as a bookmark.

Name _____

Date _____

SOLVE THE MAZE

Help the stegosaurus find her eggs in the sand.

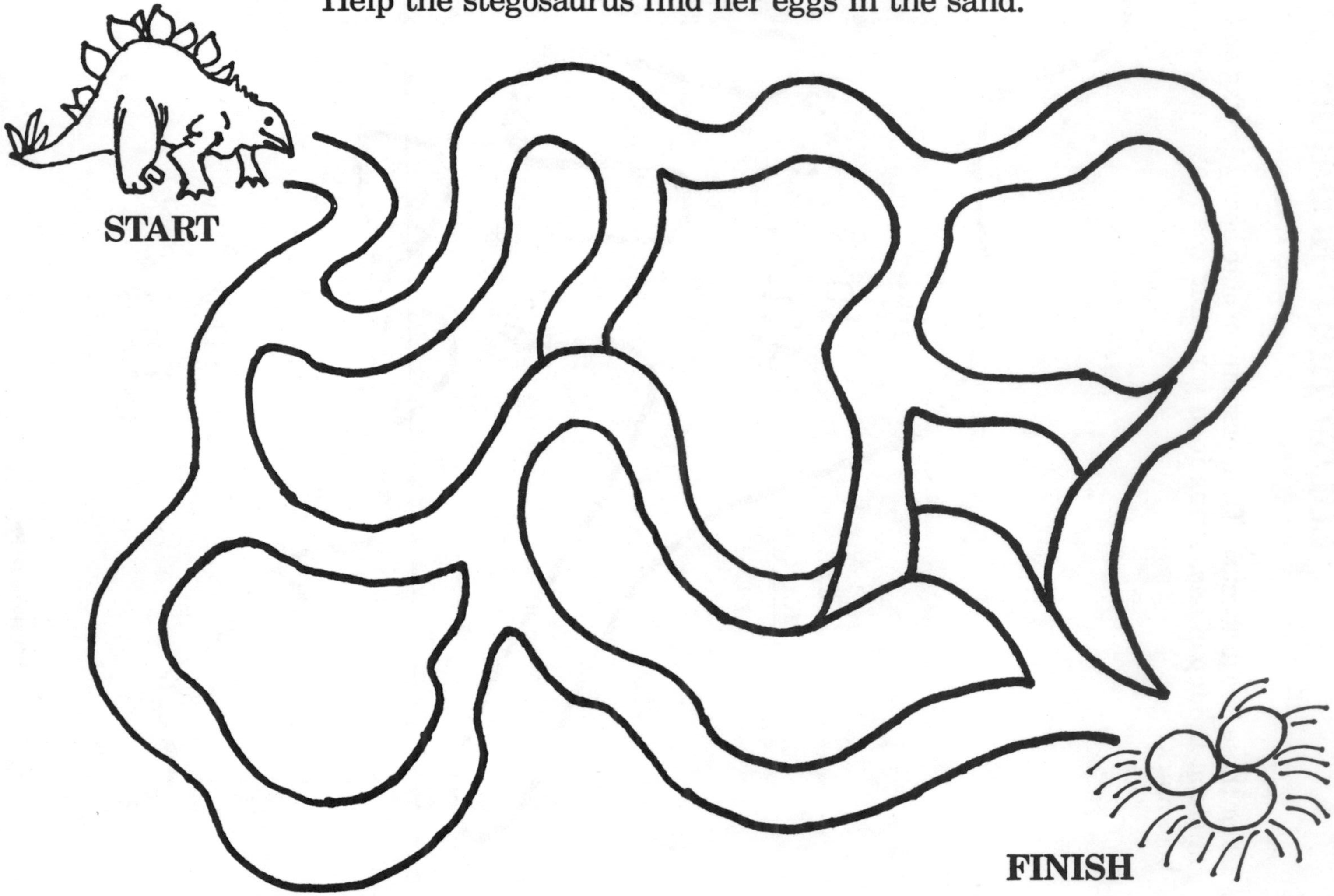

START

FINISH

Name _____

Date _____

EGGS-ACTLY TEN EGGS

Draw a line from each dinosaur number-word egg to the correct numeral egg. When finished, color the eggs.

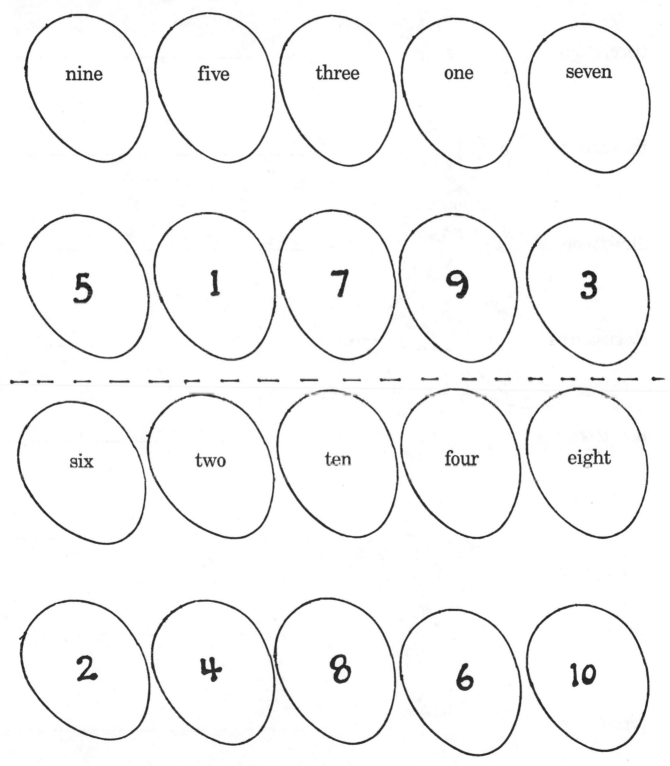

Name _____

Date _____

ALPHABETIZE THE ANCIENT ANIMALS

Listed below are eight different kinds of dinosaurs. On the lines in the right-hand column, write the dinosaur names in alphabetical order.

triceratops   _____

iguanodon   _____

dimetrodon   _____

stegosaurus   _____

brontosaurus   _____

pteranodon   _____

ankylosaurus   _____

tyrannosaurus rex   _____

Name _____

Date _____

CLASSIFY THE DINOSAURS

Some dinosaurs ate meat. Others ate plants. Usually, the meat eaters walked on two legs and the plant eaters walked on four legs. Decide whether the dinosaurs below are meat eaters or plant eaters. Color them, cut them out, and paste them in the correct column on the "Classification Chart" (Activity 2–6).

Name _____

Date _____

CLASSIFICATION CHART

MEAT EATERS	PLANT EATERS

WRITE A DINOSAUR STORY

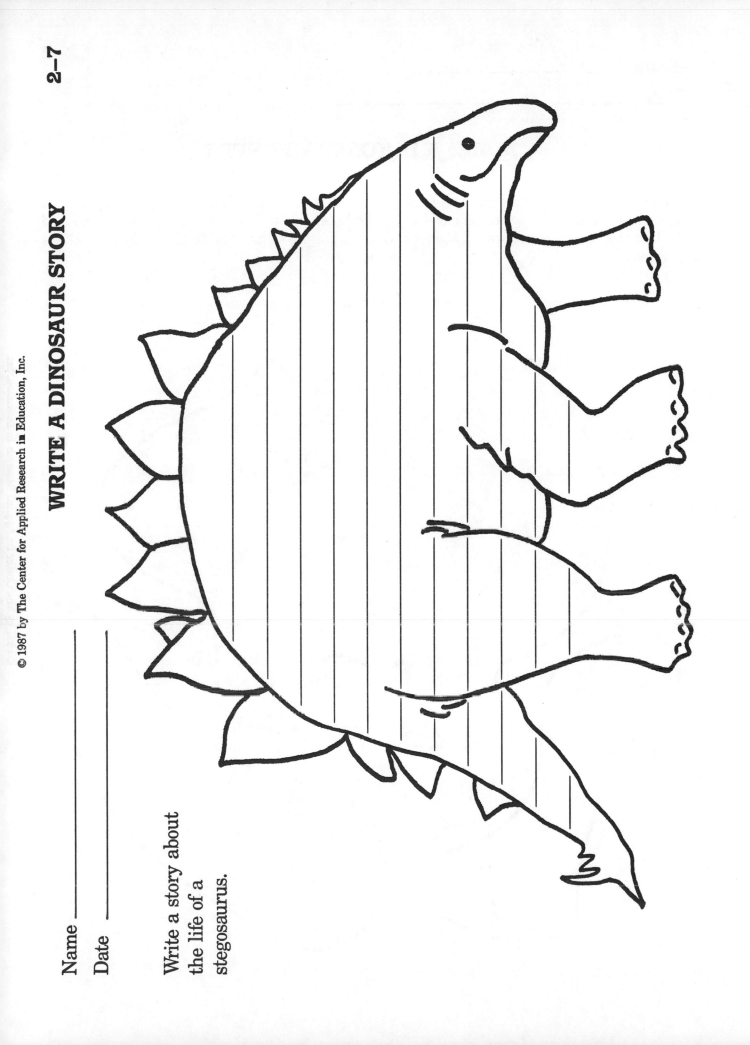

Name _____

Date _____

Write a story about
the life of a
stegosaurus.

Name _____

Date _____

MAKE A DINOSAUR PUPPET

Color the brontosaurus patterns below. Paste this page onto heavy oaktag and cut out the pieces. Use your pencil to carefully poke holes in the X's. Then attach the head and tail to the body with paper fasteners. Glue a tongue depressor to the body to make a puppet.

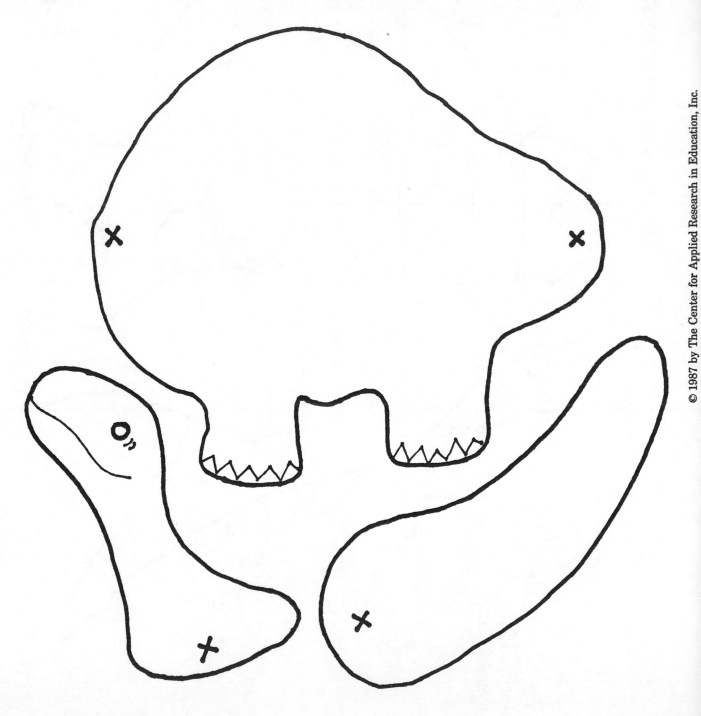

Name _____

Date _____

HOW MANY PALM TREES?

Cut apart the number sentences at the bottom of the page. Paste each one under the correct volcano and complete the equation to see how many palm trees are next to each volcano. Then color the volcanoes and the palm trees.

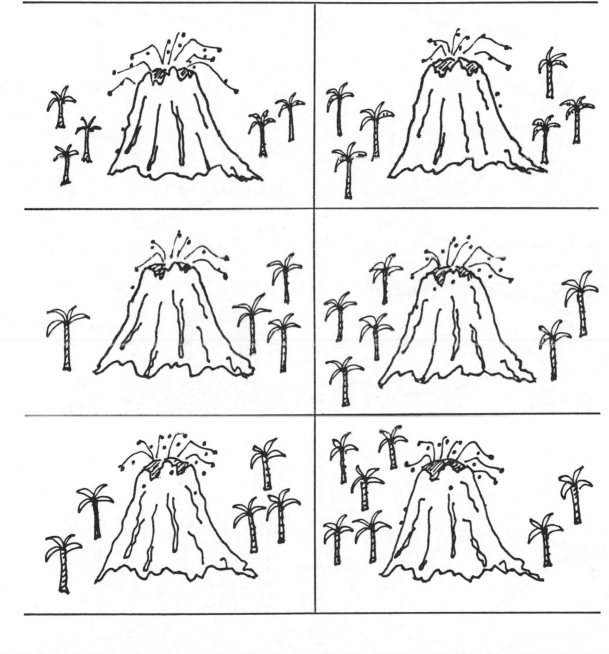

| $4 + 2 =$ | $3 + 3 =$ | $3 + 2 =$ | $5 + 2 =$ | $1 + 3 =$ | $2 + 3 =$ |

Name _____

Date _____

IDENTIFY THE NUMBERED BONES

A paleontologist is a scientist who studies ancient plants and animals. This paleontologist has uncovered some bones. She brushed them off, painted them with shellac so they wouldn't crumble, and numbered them. Write the numeral next to its number word.

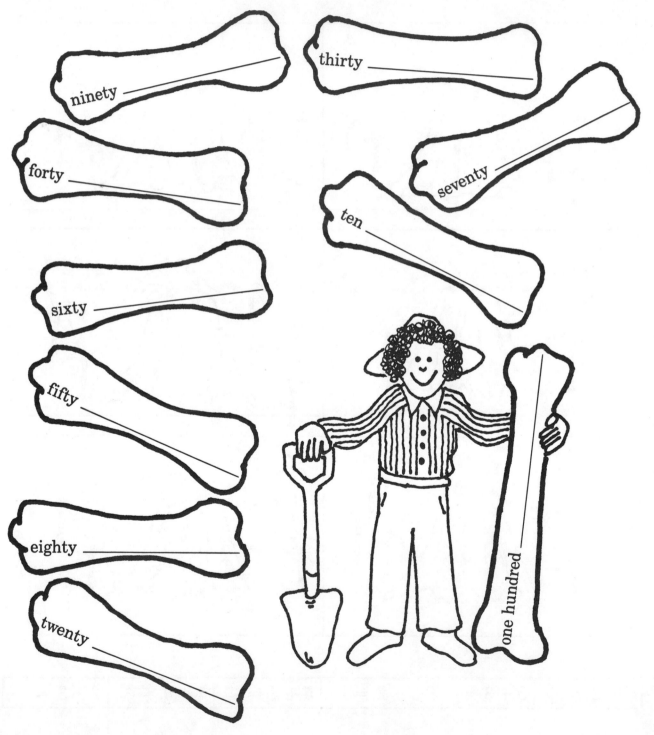

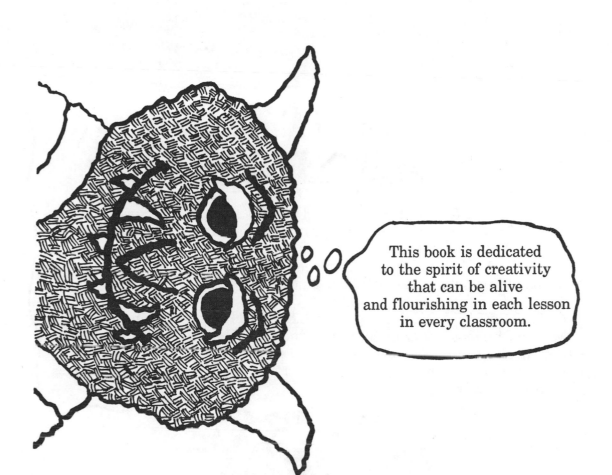

This book is dedicated
to the spirit of creativity
that can be alive
and flourishing in each lesson
in every classroom.

We gratefully acknowledge the support of Lorren, who faithfully encourages joyful expression, and Lois, who always looks to the stars.

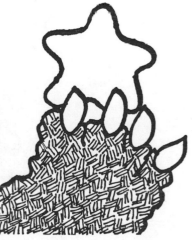

ABOUT THE AUTHORS

ELIZABETH CROSBY STULL earned her B.S. and M.S. in Education from SUNY–Brockport, with minors in English and Art. She is currently an Adjunct Professor at The Ohio State University, where she earned her Ph.D. degree in Early and Middle Childhood Education. She resides with her husband in a suburb of Columbus, Ohio.

CAROL LEWIS PRICE earned her B.S. and M.A. degrees in Early and Middle Childhood Education at The Ohio State University. She has been a preschool director, a kindergarten teacher, and taught first grade. She is currently an elementary principal in Worthington, Ohio, where she resides with her family.

Name _____

Date _____

COUNT THE DINOSAURS

The plant eaters below are hungry! Each would like to have its own special palm tree to munch the leaves. In each row, draw a line from a dinosaur to a palm tree. Then answer the questions beneath each row of dinosaurs. Can you name the dinosaurs? Color the pictures when you finish the sheet.

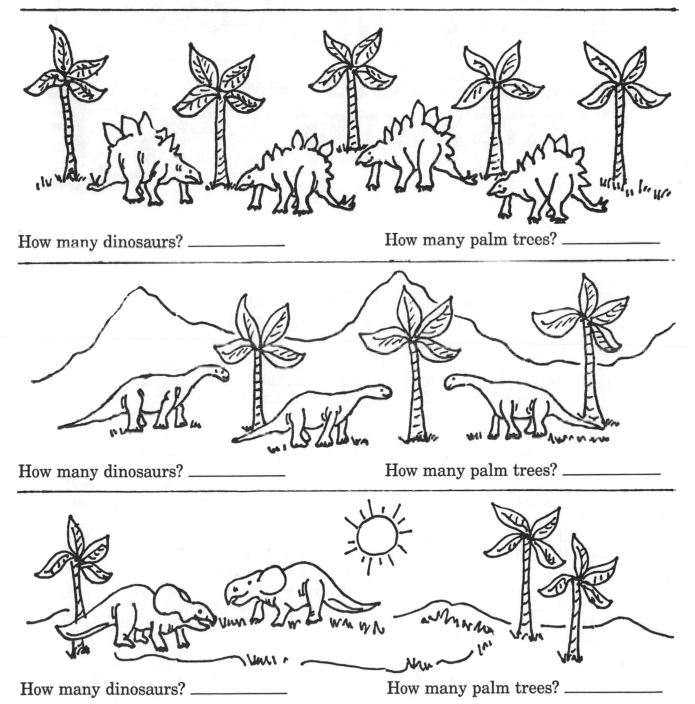

How many dinosaurs? _____   How many palm trees? _____

How many dinosaurs? _____   How many palm trees? _____

How many dinosaurs? _____   How many palm trees? _____

Section 3
CRUNCHING AND MUNCHING FRUITS AND VEGETABLES

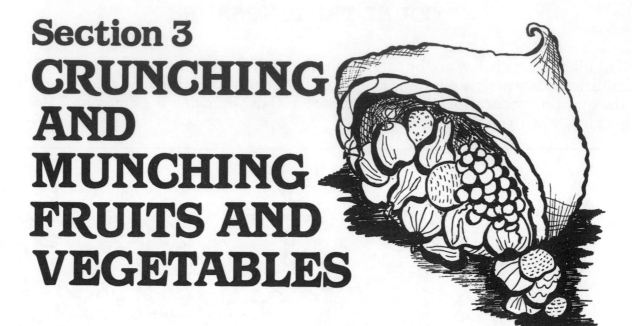

Background Ideas and Other Helpful Things to Know

Eating cultivated plants from gardens began thousands of years ago. Prior to that time, people hunted for food and ate meat, fish, and wild plants.

Then humans learned how to grow grain from seeds and vegetables from roots, bulbs, and seeds. It is not known how people learned to do this; it may have been accidental. But, they did see cause-and-effect relationships. Thus, agriculture was born. "Agriculture" is Latin and means to "cultivate the land." People no longer needed to follow animal herds and hunt. Instead, they could settle down and tend to their crops because they were assured of having an ample supply of healthful foods. When farmers did move, however, they usually took their plants (and seeds) with them.

The plant kingdom contains more than 12,000 species. Some of our plants were originally found only in Europe, Asia, or South America. It is believed that traders helped to spread the plants throughout the world.

Plants provide the energy for most of the world's inhabitants—humans and other animals, and living organisms. *Chlorophyl* (a waxy microcrystalline green plant pigment) gives plants the unique ability to utilize energy from sunlight to manufacture food.

Activity Suggestions

Nutritious Snack Week. Write a newsletter to parents explaining your upcoming fruits and vegetables unit and asking their cooperation in packing healthful, nutritious snacks for their children. Provide a list of suggestions, such as carrots, celery, raisins, oranges, apples, plums, grapes, and so on. You might want to enlist the cooperation of room mothers or the PTA for this project. The purpose of this activity is to help children form the habit of eating nutritious snacks.

During snack time, talk with the children about healthful food. Ask: "Who has carrots? an apple? celery sticks? Is it a vegetable or a fruit? Did we have more fruits or more vegetables today?" Keep a record on the chalkboard or on large sheets of paper for the week. Let the students write the numerals.

Munch-in for Munchies or Crunch-in for Crunchies. Broccoli, cauliflower, carrots, and celery can be easily washed and cut (by an adult) into small pieces and then eaten raw. Organize a vegetable get-together party. Or have a fruit munch-in. Cut up oranges, apples, pears, and so on into bite-size pieces and let everyone crunch and munch. Introduce new fruit tastes to your group by trying kiwi, mango, lichi, pineapple, pomegranate, and mandarin oranges. Discuss the students' reactions to these fruits.

"Munch-ins" and "Crunch-ins" give students an opportunity to eat raw fruits and vegetables. If the vegetables are brought to class whole and then cut up, the activity also allows the children to see what fresh produce looks like.

During this time, you might want to direct the conversation to proper table manners, especially waiting until everyone at the table is served before eating, chewing with the mouth closed, not talking with a mouthful of food, and not playing with food on the plate.

As an enrichment activity, read a storybook about rabbits during snack time and have the children pretend they are rabbits as they quietly crunch and munch those nutritious fruits and vegetables. Ask the children to wiggle their noses to signal they are finished eating, and then they may hop to their next work or play area.

A Giant Vegetable Garden. Have the children make *huge* vegetables from sturdy, colored oaktag. They can use markers or tempera paint to create a giant ear of corn, a cabbage, a carrot, a potato, a head of lettuce, a bean, peas in a pod, and an eggplant; the more variety, the better! Hang the vegetables by string from light fixtures all around the room so that the children may walk among them. (The vegetables would look this huge from the point of view of a worm or crawling bug!) During play time, let the children pretend to rake the soil under the vegetables, to pull out weeds, and to water them.

If you use colored butcher paper, cut out *two* of the same shape of the children's vegetable designs, staple three sides, stuff with newspapers (or other material), and close. These puffy, bumpy vegetables will be even more effective.

You can tie in the giant vegetables with the study or review of colors. You can also have story time while sitting around or near a different vegetable each day. Ask the children to be very quiet and imagine what the vegetables might be saying to them.

If you are working in a smaller area, you may prefer to hang the vegetables in just one corner of the room. The children could sit in this vegetable garden while looking through picture books about vegetables and farming.

Making Applesauce. This activity introduces students to measuring, timing, and seeing food change from one form to another. *Directions*: Scrub 10 to 15 medium-sized apples. Peel, core, and cut the apples into quarters. Place the apple slices in a crockpot with 1 cup of water or cook them in a heavy pan with 1 to 2 cups of water. Stir frequently with a wooden spoon. (Give each child a chance to do this only under adult supervision.) Cook until the apples are soft and mushy. The length of time will vary. When ready, cool and sprinkle with cinnamon. This recipe makes 16 to 18 full cups.

This is an excellent opportunity for many youngsters to see how something (applesauce) is actually made from something else (apples). Some children may have tasted applesauce only from a jar or a can and will benefit from this new learning experience.

Send the recipe to parents with the suggestion that it be prepared at home, with the young child as the "master chef's helper."

Food Sayings. How many sayings can your students think of that use the name of a food in the phrase? Have them think about this for a day. (They may ask adults for help.) Then list all of the sayings on the chalkboard and discuss them. Some examples are:

You're the apple of my eye.	A juicy piece of news.
Cool as a cucumber.	Sour as a pickle.
You're a peach!	Sour grapes.
Peachy-dandy.	Apple-cheeked.
As American as apple pie.	Pear-shaped.
You're the top banana.	Salt of the earth.

Vegetable or Fruit Prints. You need: 9-by-12-inch sheet of construction paper, a whole fruit or vegetable, tempera paint, a knife, long-handled easel brush, and aluminum pie plate.

Directions: Fold the paper into nine squares. Cut one item, such as an orange, in half. Place its flat side into a pie plate that contains a small amount of paint. Remove any excess paint with the tip of the brush. Place the item (orange) firmly on one of the nine squares, press, count slowly to three, and lift carefully. Repeat the procedure in every other square on the paper. This is also effective with a slice of apple, pear, cucumber, broccoli, or cauliflower.

Don't waste the edible food left over from this activity. When you are finished, some of the seeds may be planted. Some of the food can be fed to the birds, given to someone who has gerbils, hamsters, or rabbits; taken to the woods and left for squirrels and rabbits; or taken to the local zoo for the animals. Be sure that the children are aware that this food should not be wasted.

During this printing session, bring in an old pastel or white bed sheet. Stretch it flat and have the children do vegetable or fruit prints on it in an overall design. (Cabbage halves or quarters give an interesting swirling line effect.) Save this work of art for a class wall hanging, a tablecloth, or to use as a curtain to cover storage shelves (use springy extension curtain rods). The children will be proud of their contribution to the room décor.

You may also use this activity for designing construction paper book covers for any fruit/vegetable/farm/recipe/vocabulary booklets that the children are making.

Above Ground/Below Ground. We eat food from green plants. Some of that food grows above the ground (such as tomatoes, beans, lettuce, and cucumbers) and some grows under the ground (such as potatoes, yams, carrots, beets, and turnips). Create a bulletin board with pictures of fruits and vegetables. Then, make flaps from construction paper and staple them over the pictures. Have the children lift the flaps to peek for "above/below" verification. The cover of the flap could have a small child-drawn picture of the item to be found underneath, and the flip side could show whether it grows above or under the ground, either by using the actual words or by a line drawing.

Play "Above Ground/Below Ground." Call upon one child to wear a big straw hat and to use the yardstick or pointer to point to a square and say the name of the fruit or vegetable. That same child then calls upon a classmate to say whether the food grows above or below the ground. Give hints so that the game is played in a relaxed atmosphere. The child called upon then takes a turn with the straw hat and pointer. Repeat.

Stuff a Giant Scarecrow. Have the children bring in old clothing such as a flannel shirt, old jeans, kerchief, straw hat, and garden gloves. Have them make the head from a paper bag stuffed with paper scraps and stuff the clothing with paper. Prop the scarecrow against the bulletin board with the help of the stapler, or hang it on a clothes tree or a wooden cross-shape dowel structure. The children can name the scarecrow and during exercise time can flip and flop their arms and legs doing the "Scarecrow Dance." Remind the students that in order to be a good scarecrow, one must be quiet when the breeze is not blowing, become lively when the wind starts up, and then become limp again when the wind dies down.

Set the scarecrow under a large table and let the children sit under there, too, to read to the scarecrow.

Growing Plants. Grow a sweet potato vine or an avocado plant. Place the sweet potato or unprocessed avocado seed in a container of water and watch what grows. (Be patient—this may take awhile.) Also try this with carrot, beet and turnip tops by cutting off the end to allow roots to reform. Compare the rate of growth of the various plants and the size and shape of the leaves. Remember, these plants need plenty of light and warmth.

Diary of an Apple (or Peach, Pear, Orange, and so on). Help the children keep a diary for one week and write it from the viewpoint of the fruit. For example: MONDAY—The apple is growing on a tree. What does it see? What is it thinking about? How does it feel? TUESDAY—It sees the farmer coming with ladders and trucks. What noises does the apple hear? What activity is happening? WEDNESDAY—All of the apples are picked and thrown into a basket. Does an apple get dizzy? When other apples are dumped in together, what do they talk about? How do they feel? THURSDAY—Bushels and bushels of apples are traveling over bumpy roads in a truck that's closed up. Can the apples breathe? How does it feel to get jostled? Do they have to say "excuse me" every time they bump one another? Are some happy? sad? frightened? FRIDAY—The big door of the truck is opened and the apples are taken out into the bright sunlight. For awhile they can't see anything, then they see some letters that spell M-A-R-K-E-T. What do they see happening? SATURDAY—There are so many people walking by. Some stop and touch the apples. What are the apples thinking today? Do they like the looks of the people who are taking them away in bags? SUNDAY—The apples are in a kitchen. What happens? What would the apples say?

Make a Shape Book. From two pieces of construction paper, cut out the shape of a fruit or vegetable. Trace and cut several sheets of white paper and staple them between the construction paper covers. The students now have a shape book. Guide them in researching and writing factual information about the particular fruit or vegetable, or writing a creative (fantasy) story.

Weighing In. You need a scale, assorted fruits and vegetables, felt pen, and chart paper. *Directions*: Weigh each item singly. Make a chart showing a picture of the item and the number of pounds and ounces. When you have established how much each item weighs, start looking around the room to see how many things you can find that weigh exactly the same. Keep a list of your items, either by writing down the name or by drawing a picture or both. (You may want to find three or four things that weigh the same *prior* to introducing this activity to your class.)

Imbibition. A dry seed will not germinate; it needs water. The process of taking in water by a seed is scientifically referred to as "imbibition." For experimental purposes, sprinkle grass seed on a dry sponge and then on a wet sponge that is in a shallow pie plate with one-inch of water in it. Label your sponges and keep a record of what is taking place on each sponge.

Help the children to learn the new word, "imbibition." Perhaps lining up for a drink of water becomes a time when we are all seeds ready to "imbibe"—or to drink water that will be absorbed into our system so that we will keep healthy. (NOTE: Recently, several hundred-year-old lotus seeds have been allowed to imbibe and fresh green plants have resulted!)

Peanuts. The peanut is a member of the pea family. In some areas, peanuts are called "goober peas." There is a trememdous number of uses for the peanut (perhaps peanut butter is a favorite among the children). Peanuts and shells are also used in such nonfood products as paper, ink, cosmetics, shampoo, shoe polish, and insulation. The school library or public library would serve as excellent resources for peanut research. Two men whose names are associated with the peanut are George Washington Carver (he found more than 300 uses for the peanut—see how many your students can learn about) and Jimmy Carter (a peanut farmer who became president of the United States).

The A, B, C, D, E, G, H, K, P's of Vitamins. *Vita* is the German word for "life." Children can do research reports on vitamins. Ask: "What is a vitamin?" "In what foods are they found?" "If we don't get enough of these nutrients in our bodies, what deficiencies result?" Guide the children in making giant letters for the vitamins and writing the information directly onto them.

Activity Sheets for
CRUNCHING AND MUNCHING
FRUITS AND VEGETABLES

Name _____

Date _____

FOUR FRUITY FRUITS

Can you name the four fruits below? Which one's name is also its color? Have you tried all of these fruits? How do they taste? Which one is your favorite? Use your crayons to color these four fruits. Be sure to press hard with your crayons so that the fruits look healthy!

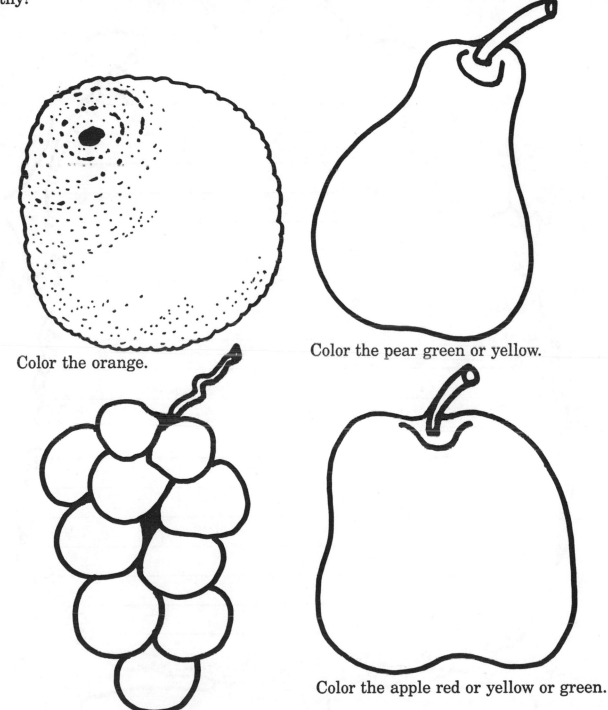

Color the orange.

Color the pear green or yellow.

Color the grapes purple or green.

Color the apple red or yellow or green.

Name _____

Date _____

THANK YOU, MR. PEANUT!

We're grateful to you for so many things. Here are just a few on my list.

1. _____
_____

2. _____
_____

3. _____
_____

4. _____
_____

5. _____
_____

6. _____
_____

7. _____
_____

8. _____
_____

9. _____
_____

10. _____
_____

Name ———————————

Date ———————————

VEGETABLE BASKETS

Complete the numeral sequence in each basket. Then carefully draw a different vegetable sticking out of each basket. A vegetable has been drawn in the first basket for you.

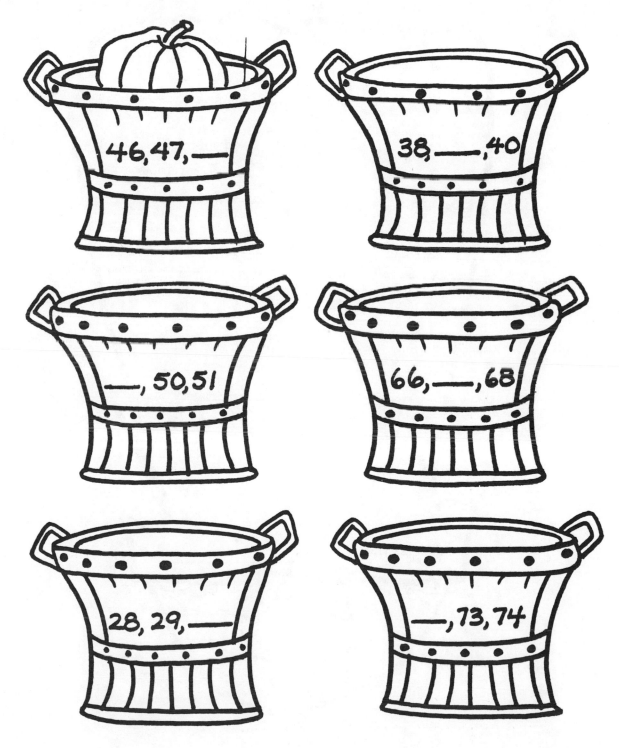

46, 47, ——

38, ——, 40

——, 50, 51

66, ——, 68

28, 29, ——

——, 73, 74

Name _____

Date _____

TRACE THE MESSAGE

Use a pencil to trace the message on the chef's hat. Then copy in the box a recipe that you helped make in school.

I am an official Chef's Assistant. I can help make this recipe.

Chef:_____

Name _____

Date _____

THE CORN IS GROWING

Measure each cornstalk. Then write the cornstalk's height on the line below.

Name _____

Date _____

MAKE A CALENDAR

Write in the name of the month in the box at the top of the calendar and then fill in the numerals in the correct squares. Draw a picture in the space provided that goes well with the month. On the back of the calendar, keep a record of how your classroom plants are growing.

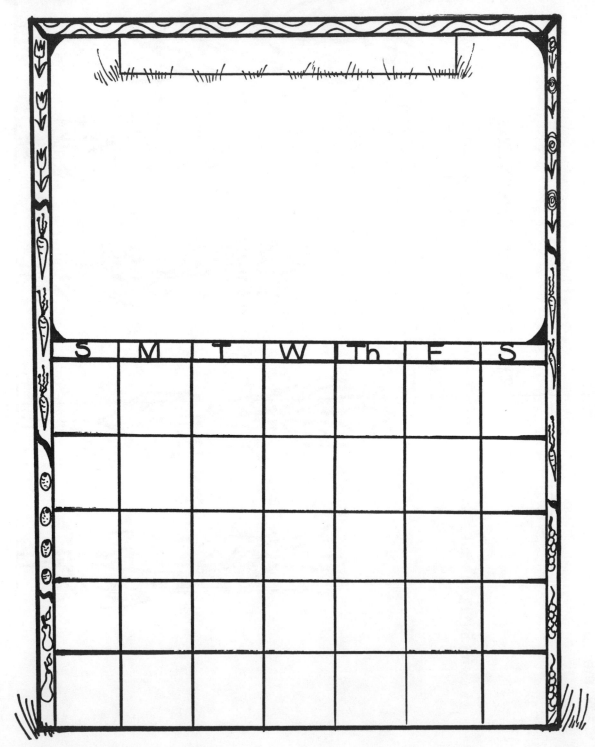

Name _____

Date _____

RECORD THE WEATHER

Weather records are important for growing crops. Keep a record for one month. Put the numerals for the days in the smaller boxes. Then each day, record the weather symbol. At the top of the page, draw the symbols you will use for Hot, Wet, Cold, Cloudy, and Windy.

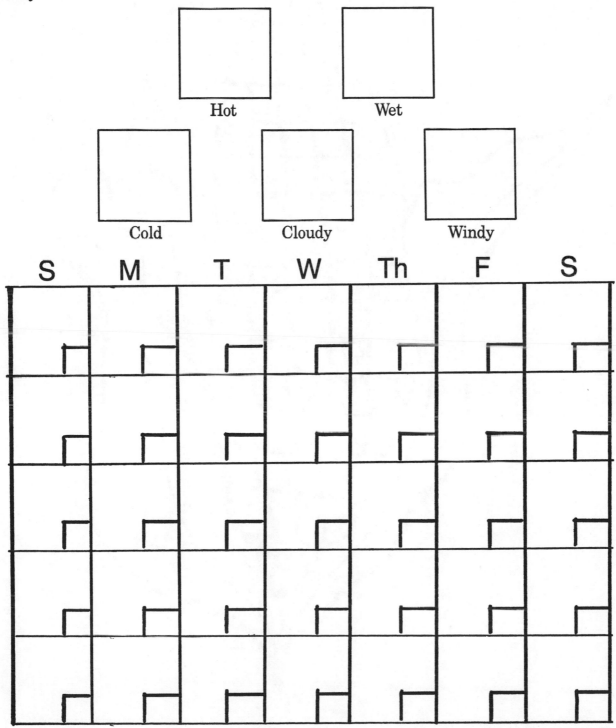

Hot   Wet

Cold   Cloudy   Windy

S	M	T	W	Th	F	S

Name _____

Date _____

COUNT THE CORN KERNELS

There are 70 kernels of corn on this cob. Write the numerals from 1 to 70. Some are done for you. When finished, color the leaves green. Then, finish writing the numerals to 100 on the back of this sheet.

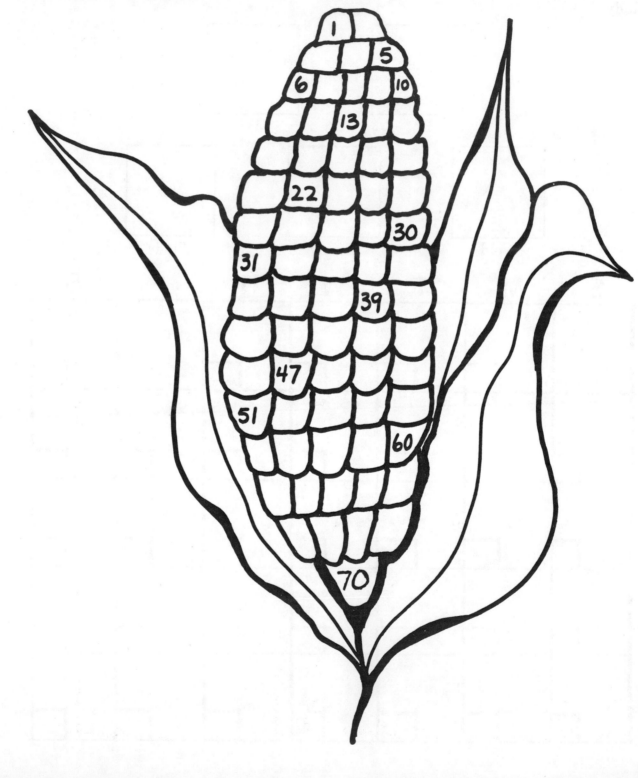

Name _____

Date _____

LET'S DESIGN SEED PACKETS

Become an advertising designer and design four seed packets for fruits and vegetables. Think about the name of your company, how to make the food look colorful, and the cost per package. Now, go out there and sell!

Name _____

Date _____

MAKE POTATO PRINTS

With the help of your teacher, cut a potato in half and carefully dig out a design. Brush some paint onto the design and then make six prints on this sheet.

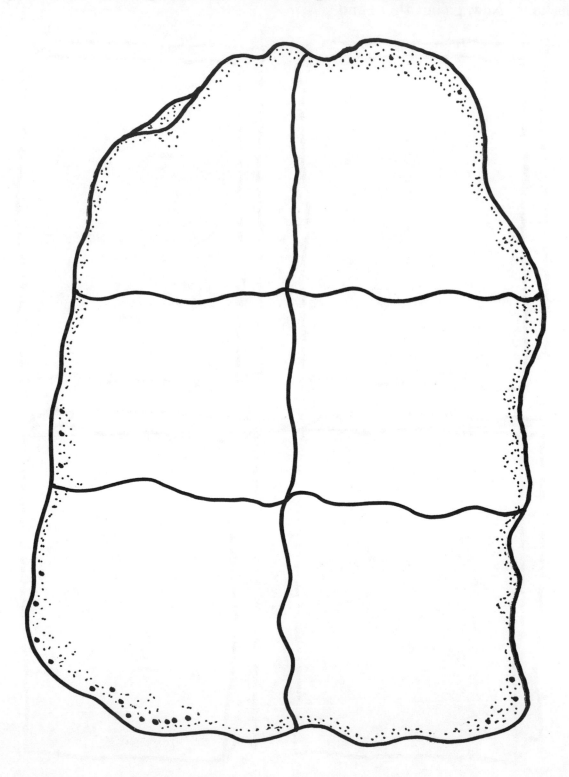

Name _____

Date _____

INVITATION TO A PEAR PARTY

Fill in this invitation to a pear party! Put on your thinking cap and try to imagine what a group of pears would do for fun. Use as many words as you can that begin or end with the letter "P."

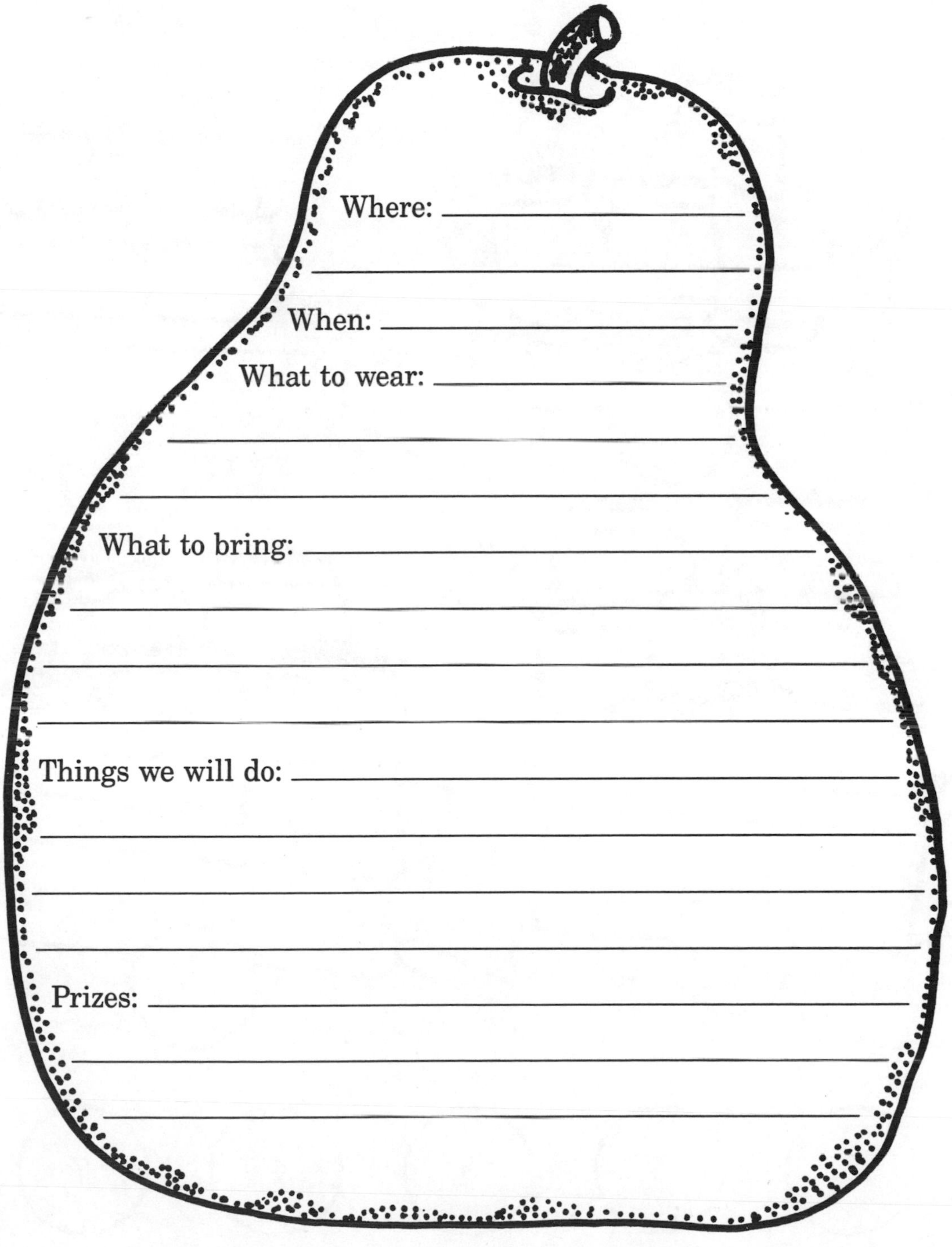

Where: _____
_____

When: _____

What to wear: _____
_____
_____

What to bring: _____
_____
_____

Things we will do: _____
_____
_____
_____

Prizes: _____
_____
_____

Name _____

Date _____

HOW MANY BASKETS?

How many baskets does the farmer have in each cart? Find the correct numeral in the circle at the bottom of this page. Cut out the correct circled numeral and paste it on the wheel of the cart. When finished, make colorful decorations on the carts. The first cart has been decorated for you.

Section 4
INTRIGUING INSECTS

Background Ideas and Other Helpful Things to Know

Insects are small, six-legged animals, and include bees, ants, wasps, moths, butterflies, ladybugs, fireflies, flies, and termites. Insects live almost everywhere on earth, from steamy jungles to cold polar regions.

Some insects help people by pollinating crops and flowers, giving us honey, and serving as food for birds and fish. Some insects harm people by biting us and our pets, spreading disease, and eating our plants and crops.

The body of an insect is divided into three parts: the head, the thorax (or middle body), and the abdomen. The word *thorax* comes from the Greek word meaning "chest" or the breastplate that protected a gladiator's chest.

NOTE: Spiders are *not* insects. They have eight legs instead of six, two main body parts instead of three, and do not have wings and antennae.

Insects are fascinating. They smell with their antennae; they taste with their feet; many hear with the hairs on their bodies; they have no voices, although some can be heard for a mile; they breathe through holes in their sides; some have no eyes while others have as many as 30,000 of six-sided lenses fitted together to form compound eyes; and many have such enormous strength that they can lift up to 50 times their own body weight.

Activity Suggestions

Insect Sculptures. Cut various sizes and colors of construction paper. Let the children roll and staple the strips to form insect bodies. Add pipe cleaners for legs and antennae, and glue tissue paper onto the body for wings.

Buggy Headbands. Everyone can be insects when they create and wear buggy headbands. Cut strips of paper two inches wide and long enough to fit around a child's head with an extra two inches to lap over and staple. Stick pipe cleaners through the headbands to form the antennae. Cut brightly colored construction paper "antennae toppers" (△ ♡ ⑥) and glue them onto the top part of the pipe cleaners.

Lists. Guide the children in making a list of helpful insects and what they do for us, a list of harmful insects and what they do to hinder us, and a list of insects that are both helpful and harmful.

Bug Catcher. Create a bug catcher from two small, flat cans (tuna fish or cat food) and a piece of 8-by-12-inch small gauge screen. Spray paint the outside of the cans if you want. Pour plaster of Paris into the bottom can. Stick a twig into the center of the plaster and place the screen around the inside edge of the can. Use the second can as the cover. (Be sure to return the insects to the outdoors when this activity is completed.)

Be a Bug. Have the children sit in a circle on the floor. Turn out the lights and ask everyone to close their eyes and pretend to be a bug inside a juicy watermelon. Ask: "How does it taste inside your new home?" "What are these hard things you're running into in here?" "What does it smell like in this watermelon?" When the children have opened their eyes, explore the following:

- Think of words that describe the inside of the watermelon.
- Cut green, white, red, and black paper and make a slice of watermelon. Label the parts (rind, meat, seeds) of the watermelon.
- Discuss how watermelons grow. Ask: "What other fruits grow on vines?"
- Talk about estimation and making a good guess. Write estimations of the weight of a real watermelon in the classroom on a green paper watermelon. Leave the real watermelon and bathroom scales handy where each child can feel how heavy the watermelon is and then weigh it sometime during the day. Gather the class together at the end of the day to weigh the watermelon and to see if any estimations are correct. (Be prepared if the watermelon should be dropped accidentally. Make light of the situation!)

- The next day, have the children estimate the circumference of the watermelon by cutting a piece of yarn that they think will fit around the melon and taping their yarn to the chalkboard or wall. The yarn can be identified if each student writes his or her name on the piece of tape. Measure the watermelon at the end of the day and decide which piece of yarn is the most accurate length. Measure that piece of yarn with a yardstick.

- When you're finally ready to slice and eat the watermelon, have each child estimate how many seeds will be in his or her piece. Save the rind and make candied watermelon rind by following this recipe: Cut apart the green skin and red meat. Cut the rind into strips, cover with water, boil for 20 minutes. Drain. Measure sugar in equal parts with the rind. Cook the peel, adding a little water only if necessary, until all the sugar has been absorbed. Shake the pot often so that the rind will not burn. Cool the peel and spread the pieces out to dry. Store in a covered container.

A Bug's Life on a Leaf. Have each child draw a picture of a bug on a huge leaf. The details of the leaf can be carefully illustrated. Guide the students in writing stories about the feelings of the bug as it sits on the leaf.

How Insects Move. Together with the children, write a list of words that describe the ways in which insects move. Let the students investigate such insects as water spiders (although not actually an insect), cabbage moths, fleas, bumblebees, ticks, locusts, and ants.

The Grasshopper Jump. This is a creative movement activity to be read and directed by you:

Roll your eyes and look around.

Wiggle your nose, up and down.

Now, JUMP, JUMP, JUMP.

Touch your elbows to your waist.

And rub your hands in great haste.

Now, JUMP, JUMP, JUMP.

Bend your knees, way down low.

Now leap up high and off you go—

JUMP, JUMP, JUMP, JUMP.

Insects That Light Up the Sky. Fireflies are beetles that glow like sparks of fire in the dark. Another name for fireflies is "lightning bugs." One common firefly is about one-half inch long, and black with red and yellow spots. It is usually seen in the summer. The firefly's light is caused by the combination of five chemicals in the insect's body. It flashes its light in order to attract other fireflies. Discuss with the students other sources of light (stars, candles, flashlights, matches, fireplaces, and street lights). Ask: "Which sources require electricity to produce their brightness?" Talk about why stars glow.

Help the children design a mural that depicts many sources of light.

Ants on a Log. Chocolate-covered grasshoppers and ants are not nearly as well received as these tasty treats! Let the children make these snacks by spreading pieces of celery with peanut butter. Add raisins on top of the peanut butter to make "ants on a log."

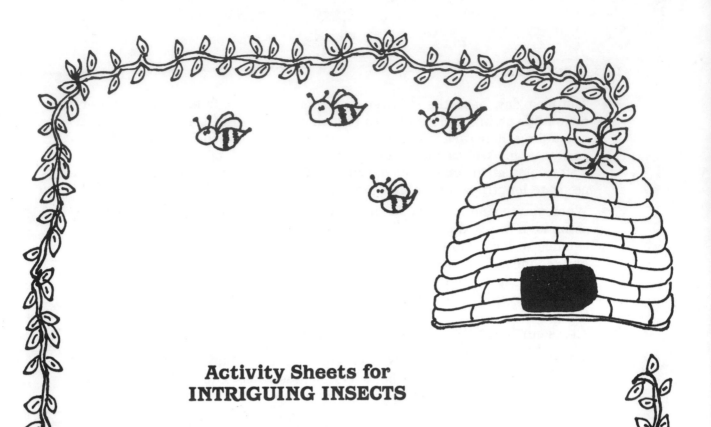

Activity Sheets for
INTRIGUING INSECTS

THE BODY OF AN INSECT

Cut out the words at the bottom of the page and paste each one next to the correct insect body part.

Name

Date

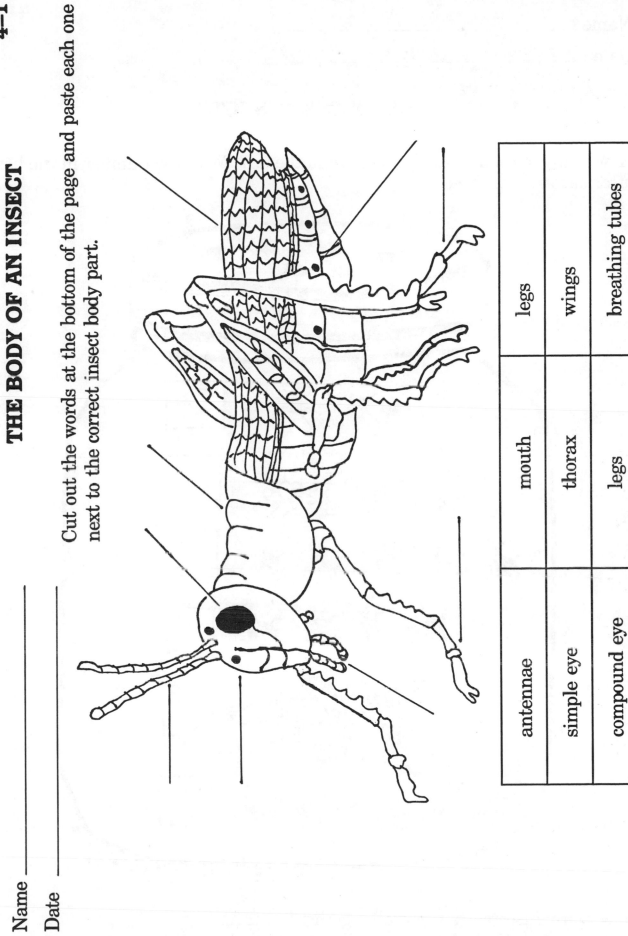

antennae	mouth	legs
simple eye	thorax	wings
compound eye	legs	breathing tubes

Name _____

Date _____

COUNT THE INSECTS

How many of each kind of insect are in the jar? Write the number in the box after each row of insects.

How many insects are there all together? _____

Name _____

Date _____

THE SOUNDS OF INSECTS

Here is a list of words describing the sounds that insects make. How many more can you think of? How many of these sounds can you imitate?

whirring
buzzing
peeping
chirping
fluttering
clicking

_____
_____
_____
_____
_____
_____
_____
_____
_____

··chirp··chirp ··chirp ··chirp

Name _____

Date _____

IF I WERE AN INSECT...

Complete this story. Make a 🐛 at the end of each sentence.

If I were an insect, I'd like to be a...

_____
_____
_____
_____
_____
_____
_____
_____
_____
_____
_____
_____
_____
_____
_____

Name _____

Date _____

THE ANNUAL INSECT PICNIC

Complete this picture of the annual insect picnic. Draw how six different insects act at a picnic. Show what they eat.

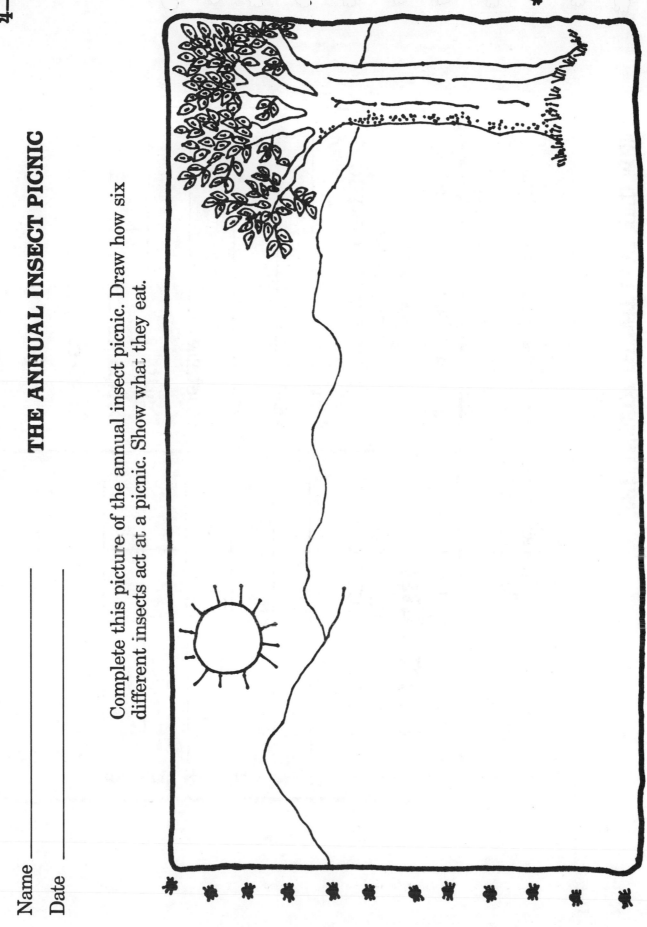

Name _____

Date _____

THE INSECT GUEST LIST AND MENU

Write the names of the six insects attending the annual insect picnic.
Then write what food is eaten.

Guest List
FOR THE
ANNUAL INSECT PICNIC

1. _____
2. _____
3. _____
4. _____
5. _____
6. _____

Menu
FOR THE
ANNUAL INSECT PICNIC

Soup: _____

Salad: _____

Entrée: _____

Vegetable: _____

Fruit: _____

Drink: _____

Dessert: _____

Name _____

Date _____

MATCH THE LADYBUGS

Draw a line from the ladybug on the left to its twin on the right. Color each set of twins a different color. Be careful!

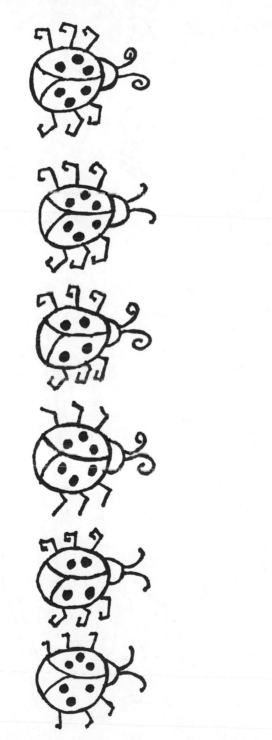 

Name _____

Date _____

COLORFUL INSECTS AND FLOWERS

Color these insects and flowers using this code:

1–green
2–red
3–yellow
4–orange
5–blue
6–purple
7–brown

Name _____

Date _____

ADD THE BEES

Cut apart the number sentences at the bottom of the page and paste each one under the correct beehive. Then complete the equations and color the bees and hives.

| 3 + 3 = _____ | 2 + 5 = _____ | 4 + 5 = _____ | 4 + 6 = _____ |
| 4 + 4 = _____ | | 3 + 2 = _____ | |

Name _____

Date _____

MATCH THE INSECTS AND NUMBER WORDS

Draw a line from each row of insects to the correct number word on the right. When finished, color the insects.

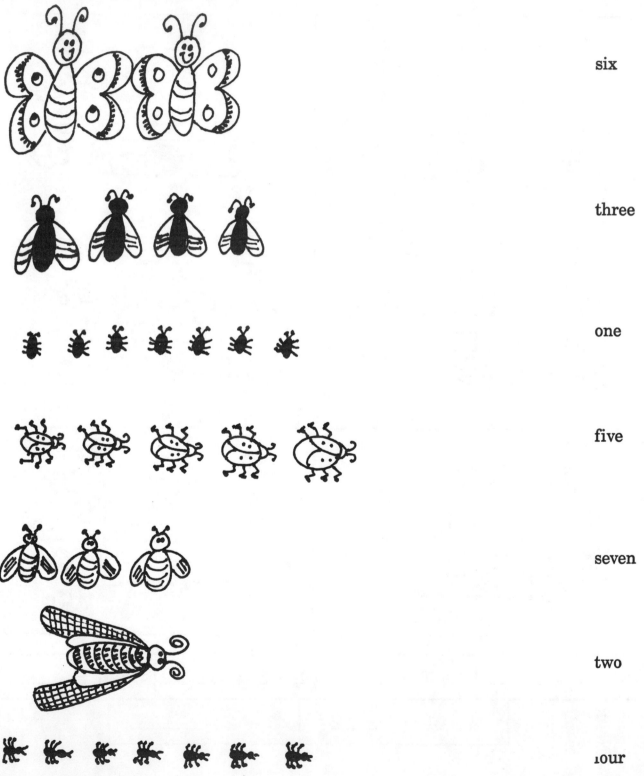

six

three

one

five

seven

two

four

Name _____

Date _____

HOW LONG ARE THE CATERPILLARS?

Measure the caterpillars before they become butterflies. Use a ruler to measure each caterpillar and then write the correct number of inches in the box. When finished, decide which caterpillar is the longest and which is the shortest.

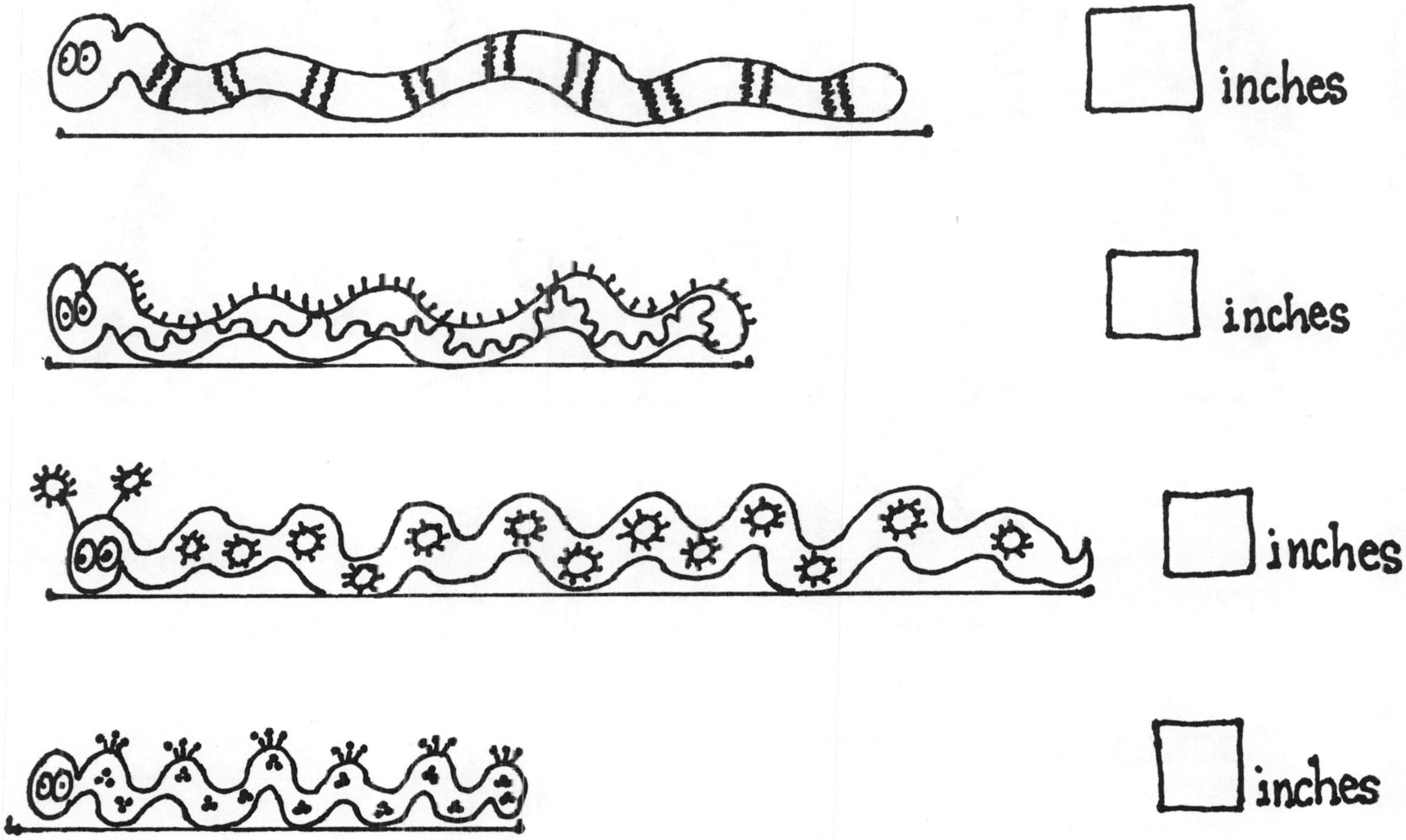

[ ] inches

[ ] inches

[ ] inches

[ ] inches

Name _____

Date _____

WATERMELON WORDS

This little insect just finished lunching on a juicy slice of watermelon, counting the seeds while eating. Now the insect wants you to write the correct numeral under each seed. Color the picture when finished.

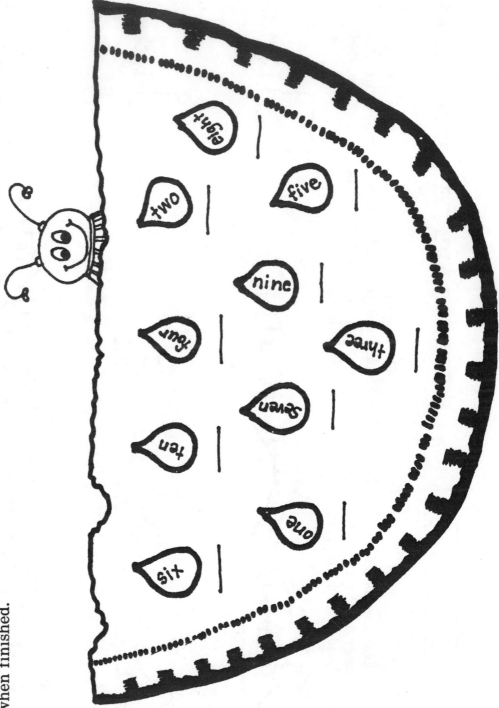

Section 5
CAREERS IN MATH AND SCIENCE

Background Ideas and Other Helpful Things to Know

Today, careers in math and science are open to everyone. Stereotypes are being broken down. In the past, often only men chose careers that required a working knowledge of math and science. Now, however, both men and women can pursue these careers.

There are many careers that require a fundamental working knowledge of science or math. The physical sciences such as chemistry, physics, biology, and botany are at the core of a variety of careers. Mathematicians with a working knowledge of calculus, trigonometry, geometry, algebra, and statistical methodology often work along with scientists to form research teams.

Some necessary traits for prospective scientists and mathematicians to have include curiosity, sensitivity, and perseverance. They must also value accuracy in order to keep careful records.

- Some science careers include geologist, meteorologist, plant pathologist, astrophysicist, and soil conservationist. Some other careers that require a knowledge of science include museum curator, florist, zookeeper, oceanographer, nurse, and veterinarian.

- Some math careers include banker, economist, computer programmer, accountant, and tax attorney. Almost any other career that you can identify requires the use of math, including stockbroker, engineer, airline pilot, musician, teacher, and mail carrier.

Youngsters need experiences to lay the foundation for early science and math awareness. They learn most effectively by moving from concrete objects (actual items) to semiconcrete items (pictures) to abstractions (words or digits) and back again. Students should be able to move back and forth with ease.

Activity Suggestions

Careers That Use Math and Science. Make three career lists on separate sheets of large paper. Label them as follows: "Math Careers," "Science Careers," and "Math and Science Careers." Print the career title or use pictures that children cut from magazines. Here are some examples:

Math Careers	Science Careers	Math and Science Careers
Banker	Chemical engineer	Dentist
Financial planner	Bacteriologist	Dental assistant
Computer programmer	Polar explorer	Physician
Travel agent	Anthropologist	Chef
Musician	X-ray technician	Teacher
Secretary	Landscaper	Artist
Tailor	Florist	Pharmacist

As a variation to this activity, list ten careers on the chalkboard. Ask the students to identify how the people in these careers use math and/or science in their work. Guide the students to find out by brainstorming, by using library resources to research the career, or by interviewing someone engaged in the career.

Numbers in Our Daily Work. This activity challenges students because the children usually have not associated math or science directly with certain careers. How do the following use math or science?

Homemaker: Budgeting, planning menu, purchasing food, cooking food, purchasing clothes (size), doing laundry (knowledge of fabrics and dyes), banking, performing first-aid, being chauffeur, making repairs

Receptionist: Making inventory of stationery items, setting margins and tabs on typewriter, typing certain number of words per minute, making appointments, telephoning, using the intercom, keeping schedules

Taxi driver: Keeping track of distance, figuring gas mileage, keeping enough gas in tank, reading meter, calculating money and making change, reading maps, knowing traffic patterns (one way, six lanes, no turns between certain hours), knowing engines and car mechanisms

Other interesting careers to use for this activity include: fisherman, waiter/waitress, police officer, garbage collector, lifeguard, sports coach, and talk show host, which all use math in some way, and many use science. Thus, math and science are needed in order to function in a complex society.

Science Terms. Help the students make a vocabulary book of science terms. Have the students alphabetize them, look up the meaning, write a brief description, and use the term in a sentence. This book can be made in the shape of a microscope or a magnifying glass. Some vocabulary starters include: petri dish, culture, bacteria, virus, laboratory, label, molecule, vaccine, and incubator.

Mind Your P's and Q's. In colonial days, the innkeeper had to keep an accurate count of the pints and quarts of spirits that were sold. This is where the expression "Mind your P's and Q's" originated. Take a look at our language with your students and see how math terms have cropped up in songs, sayings, and slogans. Some examples are:

Don't take any wooden nickels.	A baker's dozen.
I love you a bushel and a peck.	Neither a borrower nor a lender be.
Inching along.	It doesn't measure up.
March of Dimes.	Money doesn't grow on trees.
A penny saved is a penny earned.	Cheaper by the dozen.
Money can't buy happiness.	Buy one, get one free.
It just doesn't add up.	Buy it on time.
Higher than a kite.	Let's take a look at the plus (minus) side.

Scrapbook of Careers for Men and Women. The latter part of the twentieth century is known as an era when women campaigned for equal rights and became more powerful as a group. New careers were opened to women, to minorities, and to men. Help the children compile a "Scrapbook of Careers." Have them select pictures from magazines and newspapers that portray both men and women in the same career, such as firefighter, attorney, politician, physician, astronaut, and police officer.

When I Grow Up I Want to Be... Engage the students in "Early Career Interest Inquiry" by finding out what different careers entail, such as amount of education required, duties, salary, and job satisfaction. Help the students write letters to people in the immediate community who are engaged in these careers and ask specific questions. (Activity 5–13 offers you a cover letter that may accompany the students' requests.) When the responses start coming to the school, addressed to a particular class member, it adds authenticity to the inquiry process. (It is also a good exercise in letter writing, rewriting, addressing an envelope, placing a stamp in the upper right corner, and mailing the letter.) Have students read the return letter to the entire group, and then display them for all to see and read.

Number Talk. Along with Circle Time each day, you can incorporate talk about numbers. Lead students in a discussion of the ways they have already used numbers today, such as getting out of bed on time, hearing the time on radio or television, catching the bus, dialing the time/temperature telephone number, drinking out of an _____-ounce glass at breakfast, eating _____ pieces of toast, and climbing up and down _____ steps.

During "Number Talk," you can count the number of students, find out how many brought their lunch, how many will buy lunch, and how many will buy milk. Find out what time it is by checking the clock, and write the time on the chalkboard by using a number clock and by using a digital clock.

This activity can also occur at the end of the day by way of review or recordkeeping. Emphasize the fact that you are processing a great deal of information by using numbers. By using a real alarm clock, you can set it for five minutes and know that when it rings, that's the signal of "time is up." (For variety, use a theme topic that requires counting or making comparisons, such as "Pets," "Zoo Animals," or "Grocery Store.")

Number Detective. Tape a large sheet of paper (that has been cut into the shape of a detective hat, a clock, or a long wristwatch) to the chalkboard. Label it "Number Detective." Every time students "catch themselves using numbers," let them go to the paper (one at a time) and record it by writing, for example, "I measured my plant," "My plant is two inches tall," "I counted twenty straws for snack," "We scored three runs at recess." The children will be amazed at the number of times they use math in a day, and will discover that math is a useful tool that enables them to get things done and to keep records.

Math Tool Shop. Make a sign entitled "Math Tool Shop" and place it over a table. Display some math tools, such as a clock, watch, ruler, transistor radio, price tags, toy cash register, coins, grocery receipts, yardstick, compass, shapes for tracing, telephone, calculator, and so on. Demonstrate the items with small groups and allow the children to use them.

Science Tool Shop. Make a sign entitled "Science Tool Shop" and place it over a table. Display some science tools such as a magnifying glass, microscope, slides, telescope, opera glasses, lever, old scale, and so on. Let the students use these tools to investigate the properties of items brought in for the table, such as seasonal leaves, rocks, living things (fish, turtle, gerbil), growing things (plants, seeds, soil, water), and other items that children can manipulate and closely examine. Keep changing the items to make the area continually interesting and challenging.

Check the Want Ads. Bring in newspapers from the local area as well as from other sections of the state and country. Help the children to locate the Want Ads. What types of jobs are available locally and nationally? Look for trends. Set up a Career Center and help the children fill out application forms for certain jobs.

Our Days Are Numbered. Another way to show the importance that numbers play in our life is to have children record the following numbers: how many people in the family, how many pets, house or apartment number, car license plate, number of bus, number of miles (or blocks) to school, a parent's social security card number, student number when class roster is in alphabetical order, and each child's favorite number.

What's the Score? Explain that if a person wants to be a sportscaster, sportswriter, coach or athlete, he or she has to learn the rules of the game, and those rules involve math. In baseball, we keep track of runs; in football, we count the touchdowns; and in tennis, it's the match. Each sport has its own language and system of counting. Guide the students in reading and researching information about sports.

Have the students become sports newscasters. Challenge them by seeing how many times they can use numerals in a two-minute (or one-minute) sport announcement. (HINT: Some teams have numerals in their titles.)

Kitchen Chemistry. You will need several clear plastic containers, water, a spoon, and a variety of items (detergent, sugar, salt, teabag, loose tea, regular coffee, instant coffee, milk, sand, and dirt). *Procedure*: Have the children make predictions before the experiment as to which items will or will not dissolve. Then fill each container one-third full of clear water and place a small amount of one item in each container. Why do some dissolve while others do not?

Change of State. To let students experience the process of "changing states" from a liquid to a solid, make gelatin with the group. This process not only involves measuring, temperature, and time, but it also tastes good!

Have students experience the process of "changing states" from a solid to a liquid by melting an ice cube in a glass of water. But first, have the students predict what will happen when the ice melts. Will the glass overflow? Will it not overflow? What does happen? Why?

Hobbies. Make a list of spare-time activities enjoyed by the group. Then, discover how math and/or science is used in each particular activity. Here are some examples to help you get started:

Fishing— time (when are the fish biting?)
           engine (gallons of gasoline)
           weather conditions
           water pollution level
           level of tide

Reading— number of pages in book
           number of pages read
           number of chapters
           number of books written by author
           process of making paper and printing book

Baseball— number of players
           number of teams
           number of bases
           number of tries to hit ball (balls, strikes)
           number of innings
           number of home runs and runs batted in
           number of stolen bases

Activity Sheets for
CAREERS IN MATH AND SCIENCE

Name _____

Date _____

MATH AND SCIENCE IN OUTER SPACE

How would an astronaut use math and science? Write your answers on the lines below. Use the back of this sheet if you need more space to write.

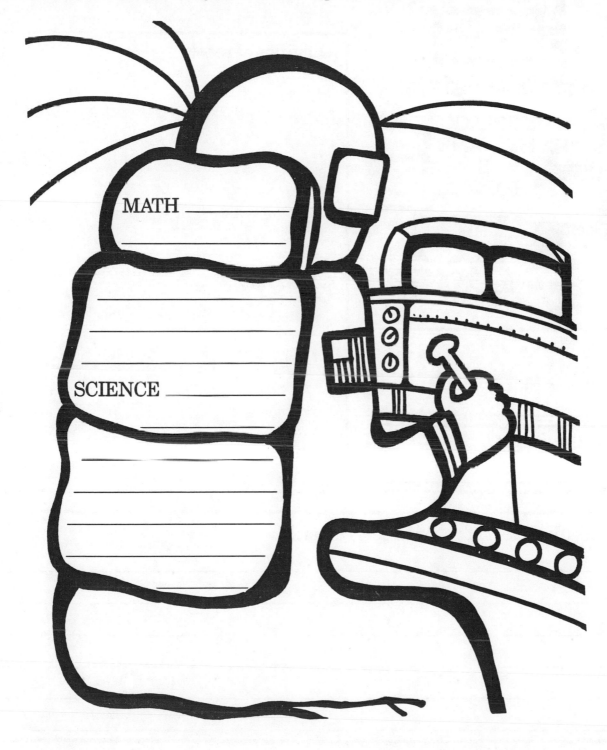

MATH _____

_____

_____

_____

SCIENCE _____

_____

_____

_____

Name _____

Date _____

BECOME AN INVENTOR

Create your very own robot with special skills for use in a specific career.

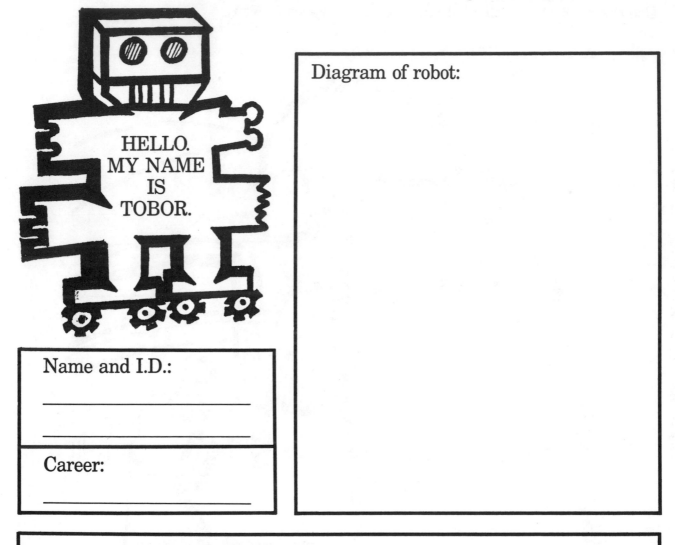

HELLO. MY NAME IS TOBOR.

Diagram of robot:

Name and I.D.:

_____

_____

Career:

_____

Specific duties of robot in this career:

_____

_____

_____

_____

_____

_____

Name _____

Date _____

WITHOUT MATH, WE'RE SUNK!

List ten ways that you use
math every day at home
and in school.

HOME

1. _____
2. _____
3. _____
4. _____
5. _____
6. _____
7. _____
8. _____
9. _____
10. _____

SCHOOL

1. _____
2. _____
3. _____
4. _____
5. _____
6. _____
7. _____
8. _____
9. _____
10. _____

Name _____

Date _____   **FACT VS. OPINION**

A FACT is something that we know for certain.
   We can prove it!

An OPINION is something that we do
   not know for certain.
   We cannot prove it!

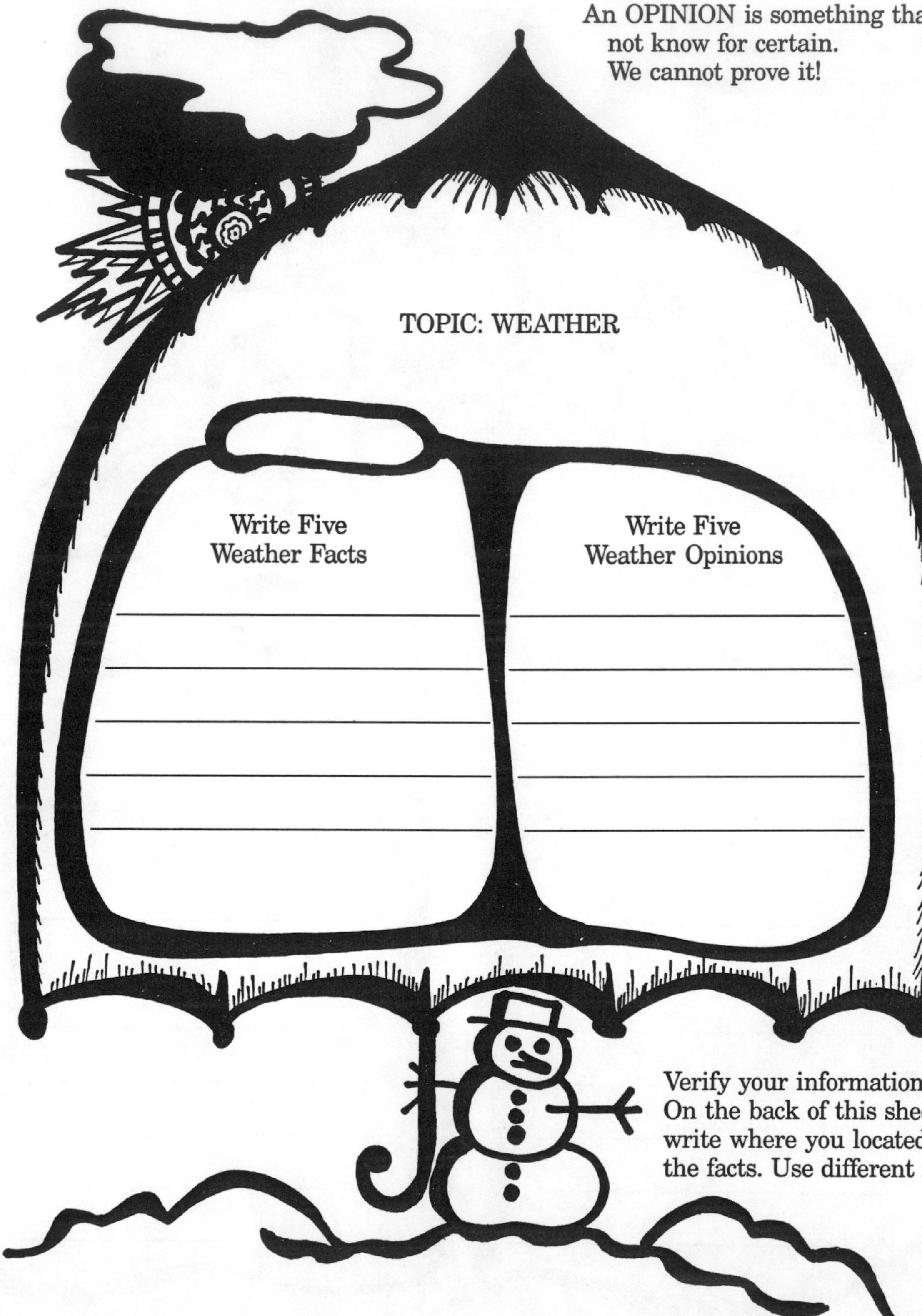

TOPIC: WEATHER

Write Five
Weather Facts

_____
_____
_____
_____
_____

Write Five
Weather Opinions

_____
_____
_____
_____
_____

Verify your information.
On the back of this sheet,
write where you located
the facts. Use different sources.

Name _____

Date _____

MATHEMATICS AT HOME

Show seven ways that math
is used at your house.

1.

2.

3.

4.

5.

6.

7.

Name _____

Date _____

SCIENCE AT HOME

Show six ways that science is
used at your house.

Name _____

Date _____

LINE SEGMENTS

Lines can be curved ⁓ and lines can be straight _____. Find all of the objects below with curved line segments. Color these red. Find all of the objects below with straight line segments. Color these blue.

Name _____

Date _____

EQUIVALENT SETS

In equivalent sets, the items are different but the number of items is the same. Match the equivalent sets below. The first one is done for you.

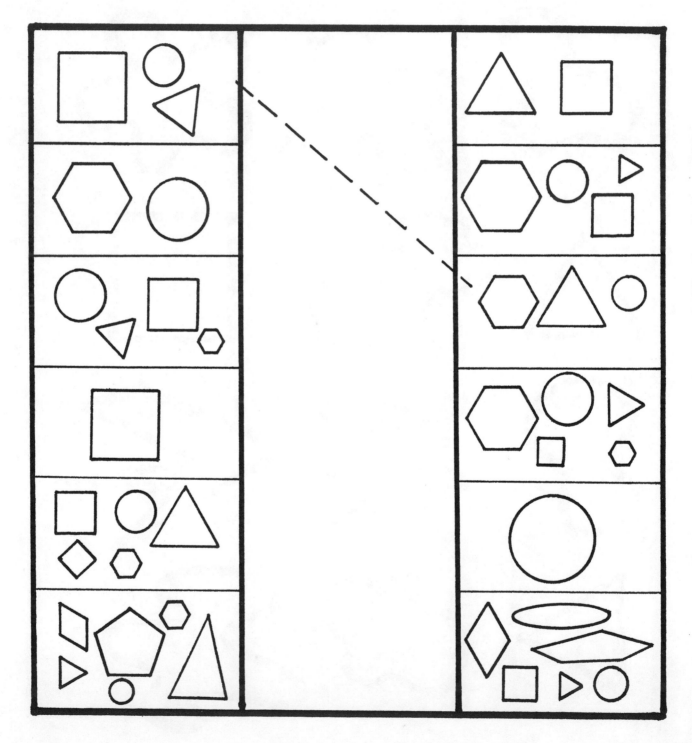

Name _____

Date _____

EQUAL SETS

Match the sets below that are exactly the same in number and items. These are called equal sets. The first one is done for you.

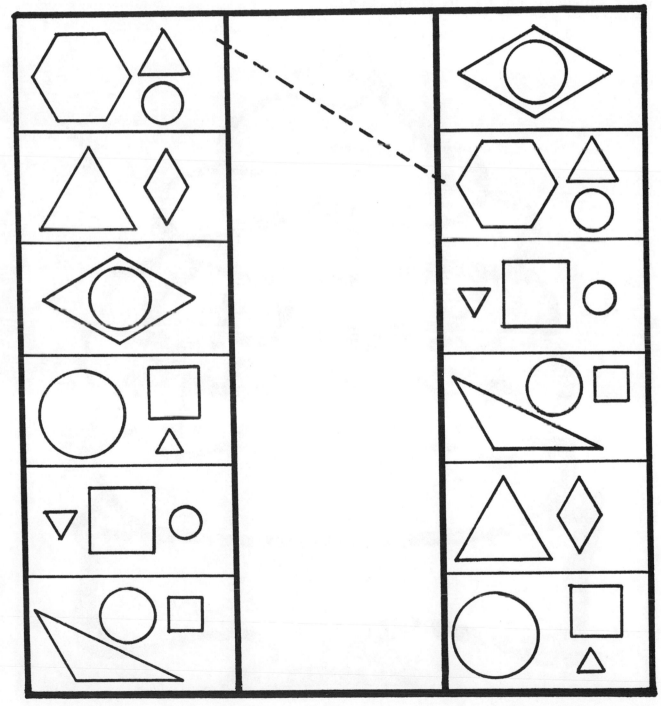

Name _____

Date _____

HELP WANTED AT THE ICE CREAM FACTORY

Create an "Ice Cream Special" that will make your company famous and will increase customer satisfaction and sales. On the back of this sheet, write a one-minute commercial (time it) for your special product. Tell the name, the ingredients, the price, and where it can be purchased. Be sure to use colorful, juicy, and appetizing words! When finished, color this ice cream sundae.

Name _____

Date _____

PUT YOURSELF IN SOMEONE ELSE'S SHOES

Select one pair of shoes shown here and write a story about the person who wore them during a successful career. Be sure to tell how math or science was used during that person's career.

Name _____

Date _____

JOB APPLICATION

Fill out the following job application. Be prepared to discuss this information in an interview setting.

1. Name: _____

2. Address: _____

   _____

3. Age: _____

4. Telephone number: _____

5. What type of work are you applying for? _____

   _____

6. What qualifications do you have for this kind of work? _____

   _____

   _____

   _____

   _____

   _____

7. Do you have any experience in this kind of work? _____

   If yes, what kind of experience? _____

   _____

   _____

   _____

   _____

   _____

8. How much money would you like to make each week? _____

WRITE TO A CAREER PERSON

_____

_____
_____
_____

Dear _____,

    Our _____ class is studying a variety of careers. Since your career is among the most popular listed by the children, a class member was chosen to write you a letter. If you can find the time in your busy schedule to acknowledge the attached letter and to answer a question or two, you would make the entire class very happy.

    Please address your reply to the student:

_____
_____
_____
_____

Sincerely,

_____

Enclosure   Teacher

Section 6
A MULTITUDE OF MONSTERS

Background Ideas and Other
Helpful Things to Know

This may be the scariest section of the book! It's all about monsters, those fanciful or frightening plants, animals, and creatures. Some of them are imaginary, like ghouls, goblins, and the five-headed monster. Others, like the Loch Ness Monster, Big Foot, and the Abominable Snowman, are considered by some people to be real. Whether real or imaginary, however, monsters have long captured the attention and imagination of people.

The word "monster" comes from the Latin word *monere*, meaning "warn." (Wouldn't we all want to be warned if there were a monster approaching!) The word "monstrous," which also comes from "monster," means huge, horrible, greatly deformed, or hideous.

Monsters are evident everywhere in literature. For example:

- Robert Louis Stevenson wrote a story in 1886 about a doctor who takes a drug that changes him into a new person who is ugly and evil. This is the popular book titled *The Strange Case of Dr. Jekyll and Mr. Hyde.*

- Many stories have been written about werewolfs, creatures that are half-man and half-beast. The word "werewolf" is of Anglo-Saxon origin meaning "man-wolf." People of the Middle Ages believed certain persons who were men during the day changed into wolves at night.

- Ghost stories usually tell the tale of the unhappy and often harmful spirit of a dead person. Years ago, many superstitious people believed in ghosts. As more people became educated, the belief in ghosts declined.
- *The Hunchback of Notre Dame* is a novel about a man who was so severely deformed by a huge hump in the upper part of his back that the townspeople were frightened of him. They didn't know he was a very gentle man.

Modern monsters include

- The Loch Ness Monster, who is reported to live in Loch Ness Lake in northern Scotland. This sea monster is supposedly about 30 feet long. Reports of the monster, which date back to the 500s, increased in the 1930s.
- The Abominable Snowman, who is a creature said to live on Mount Everest, Makalu, and other mountains of the Himalaya range of Asia. The Abominable Snowman is supposed to be a hairy beast with a large apelike body and a face that resembles a man's.

Activity Suggestions

Monsters I Have Seen. Talk with the children about the monsters they have seen on television and in the movies, and make a list of their names (Godzilla and Dracula are examples). Encourage the children to use adjectives that describe these creatures.

Ask the students to write a story about a monster, such as "The Bee That Ate New York" or "The Hen with Five Big Toes." Let the children illustrate the stories, which can be bound in book form. You might want to obtain permission to allow the students to go to other classrooms in the school and read their stories to other children.

Superstitions. Ask the children if they have heard the word "superstition" and what they think it might mean. Make a list of superstitions, including:

Step on a crack, break your mother's back.

If you drop a mirror, you'll have seven years of bad luck.

Ask the students if they believe any of the superstitions. Do they have any special objects that they feel bring them good luck?

My Own Monster. Many monsters are combinations of things, such as the werewolf, which is half-man, half-wolf. Have the children create a monster that combines the features of two or more animals or plants or people. They can draw their creatures on large sheets of paper and then write a few sentences about their monster underneath.

Monster Mash. Practice reading a recipe and measuring by making "monster mash." Write the recipe on large chart paper so all the children can see it. Monster mash is really mashed potatoes and can be prepared by using either instant mashed potatoes and adding hot water, butter, and salt, or by peeling and cooking potatoes and whipping them with milk and butter. Give each child a small plate with a portion of mashed potatoes and a plastic spoon. Guide them in using the spoon to fashion a monster head from the cooled potatoes. Decorate the monsters with pieces of green pepper, olives, pickles, dill, and parsley. Join the children in eating the delicious monster mash.

Mythology. Monsters are closely related to mythology. Talk with the children about Greek and Roman mythology (found in the encyclopedia under "Mythology") and how these mythological people are similar to the monsters we read about today.

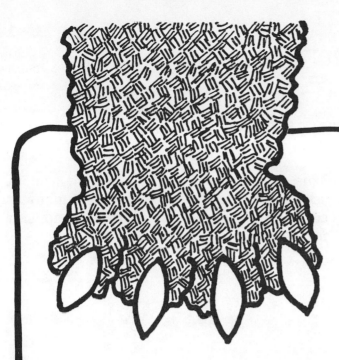

Activity Sheets for
A MULTITUDE OF MONSTERS

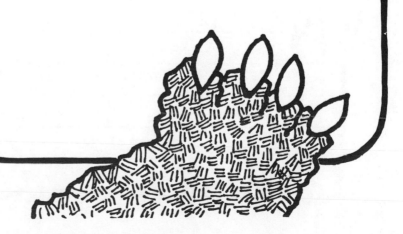

Name _____

Date _____

A MONSTER STORY

This monster would like to visit you at school. Write a story about what a monster could do in your class. Write any monster manners it may need to know.

Name _____

Date _____

SCARY CREATURES

Make a list of all the scary creatures you can think of. Some are already listed for you.

- the headless horseman
- the creature from the Black Lagoon
- slithery snakes
- vampire bats

_____

_____

_____

_____

_____

_____

_____

_____

_____

_____

_____

_____

_____

_____

Name _____

Date _____

MAKE A MONSTER PUPPET

Color this monster. Paste the sheet onto heavy oaktag and cut out the monster. Then attach a tongue depressor to make a puppet.

Name _____

Date _____

MONSTER MAZE

Help this monster find its cave. Be careful!

Name _____

Date _____

MONSTER BOOKMARKS

Color these bookmarks. Then cut them out and use them
to mark your place in monster books.

Name _____

Date _____

TOENAIL AND TOOTH TABULATION

Monsters love to practice addition! In each box, write the number of toenails, the number of teeth, and the sum of these two numbers. The first one has been done for you. Check your work!

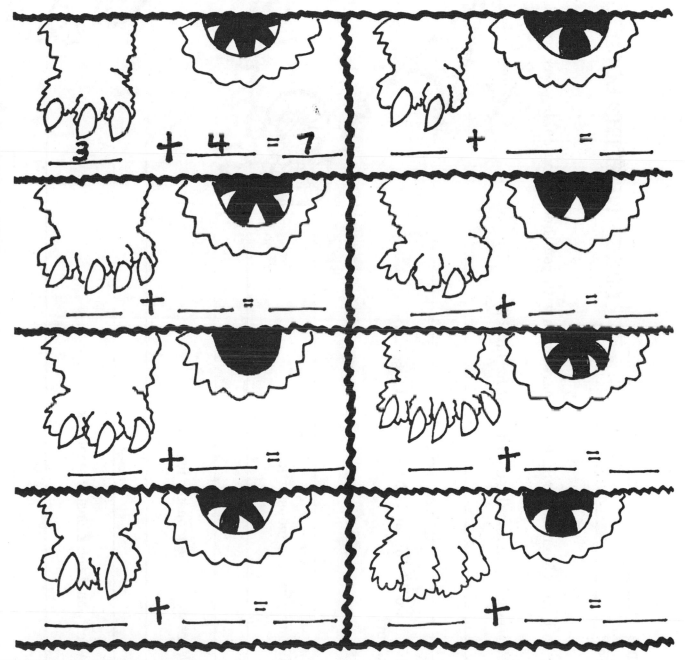

Name _____

Date _____

LUNCH WITH THE LOCH NESS MONSTER

The Loch Ness Monster would love to have lunch with you! Before you do, however, you'll have to answer these questions.

1. What would you and the monster eat for lunch?

_____

_____

2. What would you and the monster talk about?

_____

_____

3. What would the monster look like?

_____

_____

4. What would the monster feel like?

_____

_____

5. What would the monster smell like?

_____

_____

Name _____

Date _____

FOLLOW THE MONSTER'S FOOTPRINTS

The Invisible Monster is rapidly moving toward you! The only way to stop it is to write the correct numeral in each footprint. The first one has been done for you.

Now write the numbers in order on these lines.

— — — — — — — — — — — — — — **6—8**

Name _____

Date _____

MONSTER MAIL

The monster mail carrier will only deliver this monster letter if it has all of the correct information. Draw a picture of the monster sender, design a monster stamp, and address the envelope. Don't forget the ZIP Code!

Name _____

Date _____

WHERE ARE THE MONSTERS?

This little girl would like to go to sleep, but every time she closes her eyes, she hears monsters in her room. Where are they?

1. Draw a <u>green</u> monster in the closet.
2. Draw a <u>blue</u> monster under the bed.
3. Draw an <u>orange</u> monster on the chair.
4. Draw a <u>purple</u> monster beside the toy shelf.
5. Draw a <u>red</u> monster outside the window.
6. Draw a <u>black</u> monster in the middle of the room.

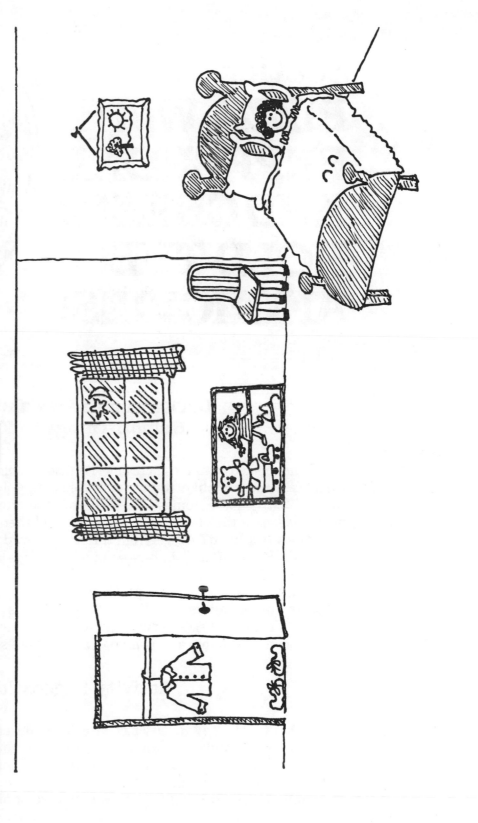

Section 7
PIZZA WITH PEPPERONI AND CHEESE, HOLD THE ANCHOVIES!

Background Ideas and Other Helpful Things to Know

When asked to name their favorite food, people of all ages often say, "Pizza!" Pizza is a spicy, pielike Italian dish consisting of a round thin layer of dough covered with cheese, tomato sauce, herbs, and often bits of sausage, pepperoni, anchovies, or a variety of other toppings, and then baked.

The word "pizza" comes from the Italian word *pesta*, meaning "thing that is pounded." Since pizza dough is pounded as it is flattened, it is understandable why that name is appropriate.

Many restaurants offer pizza on the menu and some even specialize in preparing pizza any way you like it. "Pizza pie," as it was originally called, comes in many shapes and sizes. It is a nutritious food, containing ingredients from the four basic food groups, and is a good after-school snack.

Activity Suggestions

Pizza in My Town. Discuss with the children and then make a list of the many different kinds of pizza available in your town. How many meats, fruits, and vegetables are represented on your list? Then make a large graph of the different kinds of pizza suggested in this discussion. Have each child sign his or her name underneath his or her favorite kind of pizza:

- Which pizza was the most favorite?
- Which pizza was the least favorite?
- Were there any that got equal numbers of votes?
- How many more people like the favorite pizza than chose the least favorite pizza?
- What pizzas had even numbers of votes?
- What pizzas had odd numbers of votes?

Design a Pizza Box. Many pizza restaurants have a delivery service, where you can telephone in your pizza order and have it delivered to your door. The pizza usually arrives in a cardboard box with the restaurant's name on the cover. Ask the students to pretend they are a pizza maker. Have them design a cover for the pizza delivery box that will tell their customers what makes their pizza so special.

Field trip. Arrange to take a field trip to a local pizza parlor. Talk with the owner or the chef about the kinds of pizza made, where ingredients are purchased, how workers are trained, and how they get ideas for new pizzas. When you return to school, ask each child to write a story about the trip.

Pizza for Lunch. Enjoy a pizza for lunch at school. Involve the children in measuring the ingredients and baking the pizza, using one of the recipes here or a favorite recipe of your own.

Easy Pizza. Using half a hamburger roll for each child, spread each top and bottom with a tablespoon of spaghetti sauce. Sprinkle the pizzas with grated mozzarella cheese and bake for 10 minutes in a 250°F oven.

Homemade Pizza. Sift together 2 cups unbleached flour and 1 cup whole wheat flour. Then resift with 2 teaspoons sugar and 1½ teaspoons salt. Dissolve 1½ cakes (3¾ teaspoons) yeast in 2 tablespoons warm water and then add 1 cup warm milk. Stir the liquid into the sifted ingredients. Stir in 3 tablespoons melted butter and blend until smooth.

Knead the dough into a ball and cover with a cloth. Place the bowl in a warm spot for 15 minutes. Then divide the dough in half, roll out two pizzas, and allow these to rise for up to one hour.

Spread 1 can of Italian tomato sauce on top of the dough and sprinkle with 1 teaspoon of oregano. Cover the pizzas with sliced pepperoni, green peppers, black olives, cooked meat, mushrooms, or any other combination. (Be sure to check with the students as to their likes and dislikes!) Sprinkle with grated longhorn or mozzarella cheese and bake for 20 minutes in a 400°F oven.

Menus. Visit restaurants in your area and ask if they have old menus they are willing to donate to your classroom. Using the menus as resources, guide the students in comparing prices of similar items, comparing the number of choices on the menus, comparing the cost of dinner at one restaurant with another, comparing menu covers and printing, graphing the number of times a food item appears on the menus, and identifying healthy meals. You might ask the students to then design their own menus.

Italian Foods. We know that pizza comes to us from Italy, but what other foods are also from that country? Together with the children, list foods from Italy as well as foods from other countries around the world. Make up stories to tell how and why each food may have originated in that particular country. Are there restaurants in your town that specialize in preparing foods from these countries?

Tasting Day. Discuss with the children the meaning of "heritage" (that which is handed down from one's ancestors or the past). Involve the children in discovering where each of their ancestors came from and ask them to bring a family recipe from that country. Have a "Tasting Day" at school and compile a cookbook of all these "ancestral" recipes.

Activity Sheets for
PIZZA WITH PEPPERONI AND CHEESE,
HOLD THE ANCHOVIES!

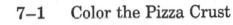

Name _____

Date _____

COLOR THE PIZZA CRUST

Here's your chance to make a pizza. Color this pizza crust brown and add the sauce and pepperoni from Activity 7–2. Draw in your favorite toppings on the red sauce. Cut strips of yellow construction paper "cheese" to cover the pizza. Yummy!

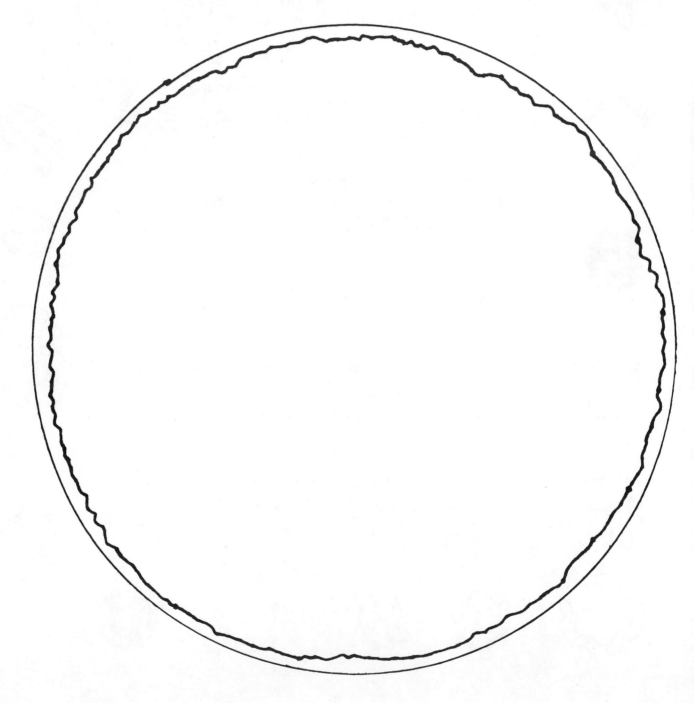

Name _____

Date _____

PUT THE PEPPERONI IN PLACE

Cut out each numeral pepperoni at the bottom of this sheet and paste it onto the correct number word. Then color the sauce red and the pepperoni orange.

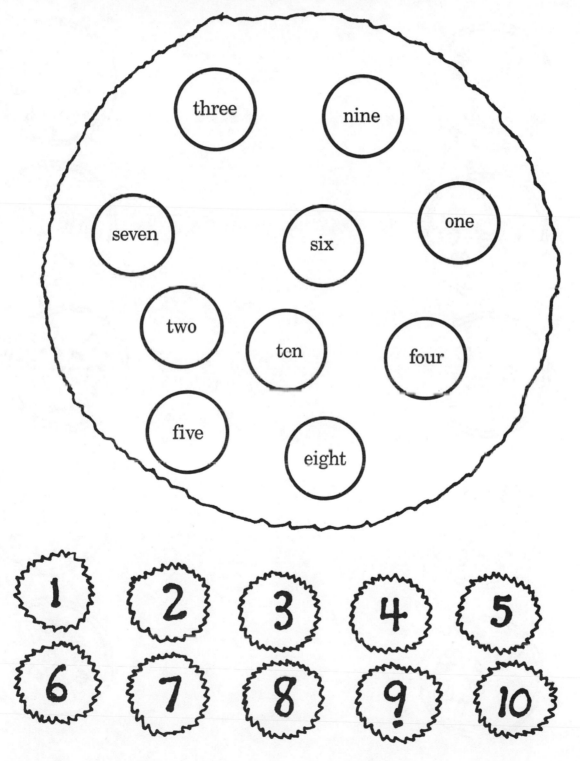

Name _____

Date _____

MATCH THE PIZZAS

Draw a line from the pizza on the left to the matching pizza on the right. Be careful!
Then color each pair of matching pizzas a different color.

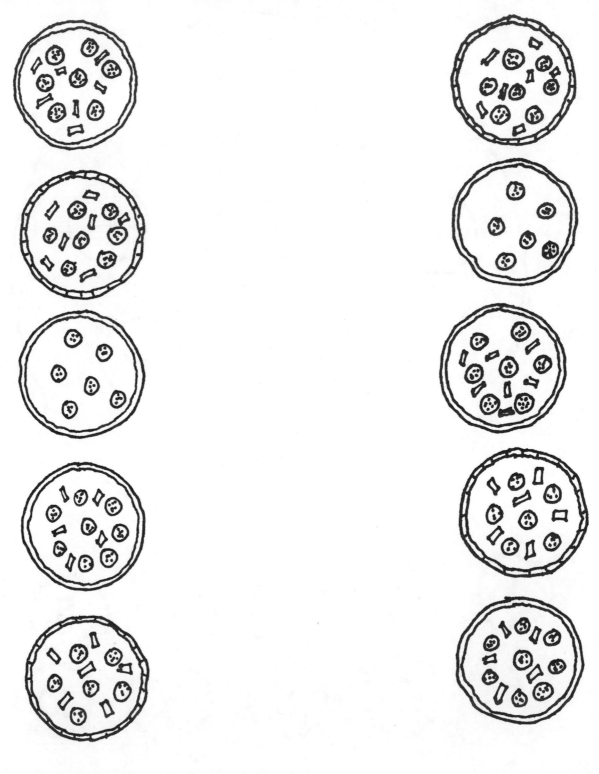

Name _____

Date _____

PIZZA AND THE BASIC FOOD GROUPS

Pizza is a nutritious food because each of the four basic food groups is represented in a pizza. Look at the pizza ingredients below and write the name of the correct food group underneath each one. The four basic food groups are:

- meats and poultry
- fruits and vegetables
- grains and cereals
- milk and dairy products

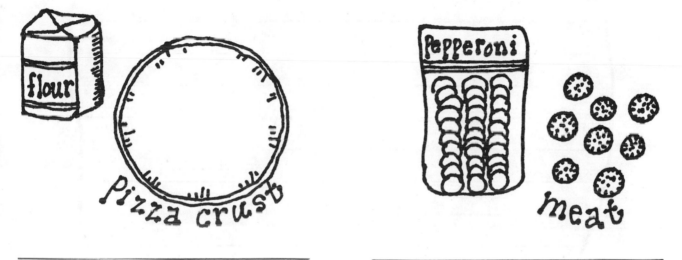

_____   _____

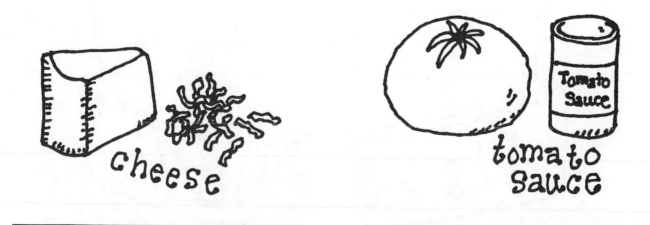

_____   _____

Name _____

Date _____

BE A PIZZA CHEF

Pretend you're a famous pizza chef. Write your very own pizza recipe that will be included in a gourmet cookbook.

My Pizza Recipe

_____

_____

_____

_____

_____

_____

_____

_____

_____

_____

_____

_____

_____

_____

_____

Pizza Chef

Name _____

Date _____

SOLVE THE PIZZA FRACTIONS

Someone has eaten part of each pizza below. The pizzas have been divided into equal parts. On the line next to each pizza, write the fraction for the piece of the whole pizza that has been eaten.

Then color red sauce on each pizza. On the pizza divided into thirds, add orange pepperoni to one-third of the pizza. On the pizza divided into fourths, add green pepper strips to three-fourths of the pizza. On the pizza divided into sixths, add black olives to two-sixths of the pizza. On the pizza divided into halves, add yellow pineapple to one-half of the pizza.

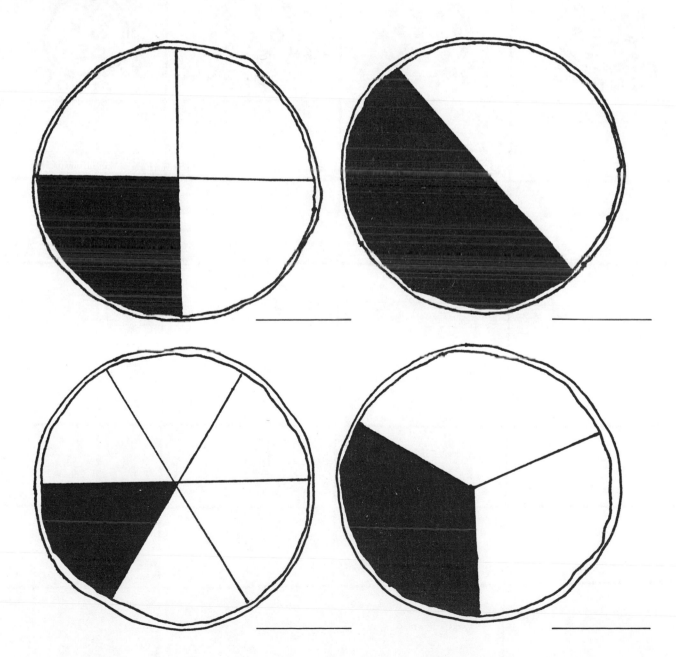

Name _____

Date _____

A PIZZA GRAPH

Ask 12 of your friends to pick their favorite kind of pizza from below. Have each person write his or her name in a box below his or her choice, starting with the top box in each column. Which kind of pizza was the most favorite? Which was the least favorite? Did any pizzas have equal votes?

Which kind of pizza is your favorite?

Name

Date

PIZZA PATTERNS

This large pizza has been cut into four rows. Each row has a different pattern of toppings. Complete the pattern in each row, then color this deluxe pizza.

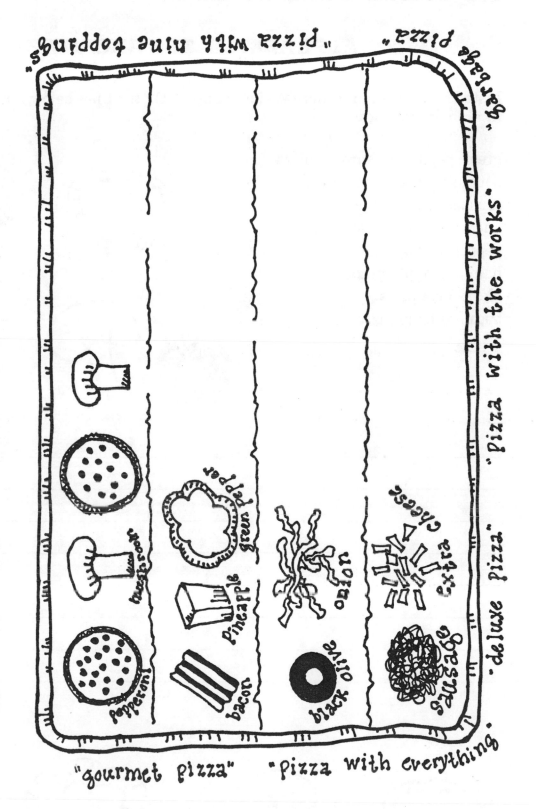

Name _____

Date _____

ALPHABETIZE THE ANCHOVIES!

Listed here are eight different kinds of pizza. On the lines below, write the pizza names in alphabetical order.

green pepper-mushroom pizza
double cheese pizza
sausage-onion pizza
anchovy-green olive pizza
pepperoni pizza
ham-pineapple pizza
black olive pizza
bacon-almond pizza

© 1987 by The Center for Applied Research in Education, Inc.

_____

_____

_____

_____

_____

_____

_____

Name _____

Date _____

THE MENU MEMORY GAME

Each box below contains a pizza topping that you might find on a menu. Color each ingredient and cut the boxes apart on the lines. To play the memory game:

- Lay the cards face down on a table or the floor and turn over two cards at a time.
- If the two cards match, keep them.
- If the two cards don't match, return them to the pile and your turn is over.
- Try to remember where each topping is hidden as other players take their turns. The person with the most pairs at the end of the game is the winner.

Name _____

Date _____

BUYING PIZZA INGREDIENTS

You must go to the food store to buy ingredients for a pizza dinner. Look at the grocery items here and then answer the questions below.

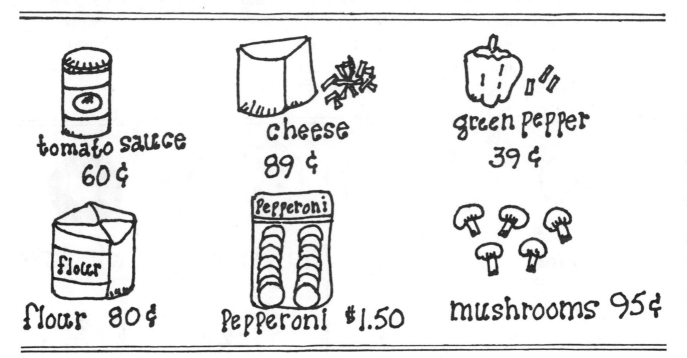

tomato sauce 60¢

cheese 89¢

green pepper 39¢

flour 80¢

Pepperoni $1.50

mushrooms 95¢

1. Which item costs the most? _____

2. Which item costs the least? _____

3. Which costs more, green peppers or mushrooms? _____

4. Which costs less, cheese or flour? _____

5. Do any of the items cost an equal amount? _____

6. How much would it cost to make a cheese pizza? You'll need flour for the crust, tomato sauce, and cheese. _____

7. If you brought a five-dollar bill to the store, would you have enough money to buy ingredients for a cheese pizza? _____

8. Do you have enough money to buy the ingredients for a cheese-mushroom pizza?

_____

Section 8
MICE AND FRIENDS

Background Ideas and Other Helpful Things to Know

Rodents belong to the group or class of animals called "mammals." Mammals are usually covered with fur or hair when born and are fed with milk by their mothers.

The outstanding feature of rodents is their front teeth, which keep growing during their entire lifetime. That is why a rodent *must* gnaw or chew to keep wearing down its teeth. If a rodent didn't gnaw and chew all the time, its front teeth would grow so long that it couldn't close its mouth. Then, it wouldn't be able to eat and stay alive. A rodent must chew, chew, chew for its very life!

Activity Suggestions

Big/Little Box. Not only rodents are big (beavers) and little (mice); other things also come in different sizes. Collect ten items in an attractive box and have the students put them in order from largest to smallest. You might also offer children a box with one item in ten different sizes, such as tiny to big buttons, stones, or stamps, to put in order by size.

Classification. You need one box with small cubicles and a variety of small items (nuts, seeds, coins, paper clips, buttons, cubes, and so on). Have the children work independently or in pairs to sort the items and place them into the cubicles.

117

Then have them draw and label the classifications on a 9-by-12 inch or 12-by-18 inch sheet of paper, and display the completed classification pictures. (Children will have a variety of ways to classify, such as by color, texture, size, use, pictures, and so on. Accept all answers as long as there is a rationale.) This activity can be repeated several times using different items.

Pawprints and Handprints. Discuss animal paws and the prints they make, and people hands and the prints (outlines) they make. Create a large chart to list ten things an animal can do with its paws and ten things a person can do with his or her hands. How many things are the same? Different? Who can do more things?

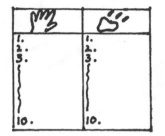

Fingerprints. When discussing paws and hands with the children, extend the conversation to fingerprints. Use an ink pad and make identification prints for each child (to take home or to keep in the permanent record folder). Also make thumb prints on small pieces of paper and create images from them. Call your local police department and ask to have an officer come to class to demonstrate fingerprinting equipment.

Most Wanted. Discuss how each fingerprint is unique, then talk about how fingerprints identify people (the FBI's "Most Wanted" list). Talk about good citizenship in your classroom and what behavior is "most wanted," such as good listeners, no shouting indoors, raise hand before talking, sharing, and so on. Get a large sheet of posterboard and print "Most Wanted" for a title. Then list the qualities that the class is looking for. Have the children press their thumb prints onto the poster and print their names under it to identify them as the children you are looking for with these good qualities.

Mouse and Cheese Maze. Create a maze on a table, countertop, or floor using long strips of construction paper and cardboard or blocks. Make a mouse from plasticene and put it at the start of the maze. Make a piece of yellow cheese from plasticene and put it at the end of the maze. See if your students can get the mouse to "capture" the cheese. Time the results. How long does it take to move the mouse through the maze? Older children can draw a maze on graph paper.

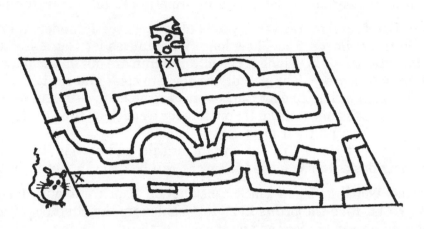

Protection in the Outdoors. Explain that a squirrel makes good use of its natural protection—its tail. A squirrel uses its tail as an umbrella in the rain, to wrap around as a blanket when it is asleep, or as a sunscreen to shade itself from the scorching hot sun.

Discuss with the children what people need for outdoor protection when they are (1) at the beach, (2) on a camping trip, (3) in the desert, and (4) in a snowstorm. Take four large sheets of paper and cut them into the following shapes: giant beach ball, huge tent, enormous sun, and a great big snowman. On these shapes that represent the four settings, have the children draw protective clothing or items needed. As an alternative to drawing, you may prefer to have the children locate pictures of the items in magazines, cut them out, and paste them on the appropriate shape.

Favorite Vegetables Book. The beaver is a vegetarian and likes to eat roots and twigs. Make a class book of the students' favorite vegetables by letting each child contribute a page. Dedicate the book to beavers and make sure a beaver is drawn on the cover. Make up a catchy title and discuss the book with the total group.

Nature's Pincushion. The porcupine, with all of its quills (or spines), has been called "nature's pincushion" because it can roll itself into a ball for protection. The spines can be as long as 20 inches! Do the children know how long 20 inches is? Have them get a yardstick and measure the length of 20 inches. Then help them find ten things in the room that are 20 inches long and write these on the chalkboard. How many things can they find at home that are 20 inches long?

Making Pincushions. In honor of the porcupine, help the children cut out two 2-by-2-inch felt or cotton squares and sew up three sides (older children can do this alone). Have the children stuff the pincushion with cotton or craft material. Enlist the help of an aide to sew up the fourth side if children are too young or if you are too busy. These pincushions can be gifts for parents, grandparents, or neighbors along with information to tell about the porcupine.

Come Up for Air. Beavers can hold their breath underwater for five minutes. Do the children know how long five minutes is? Get a stopwatch and time five minutes to see how long it is while children are out on the playground or while listening to a story. Bring an alarm clock to class and set it to ring in five minutes. The slogan "It's time for the beaver to come up for air" can be a signal to the children that it's time to be quiet or time for a snack or time to clean up their toys or time to clean up their desks.

Get a silent egg timer (filled with sand or salt) and have individual children take it to their desks to see how much work can be done in five minutes.

Creative Writing. From black construction paper, cut out at least eight large paw prints. Tape the prints in zigzag fashion up the chalkboard and into a roll-up map, or across the floor and up the wall to the ventilator, or across the floor and up the wall into a cupboard. Can the children tell who this classroom visitor was? What can we tell by the prints? What did it see in the room? What did it do? Where did it go? Have the children write about the mysterious visitor on paper in the shape of a large paw print. (After you have used paw prints, repeat this with cutouts of hoof prints and footprints.)

Equal Parts. A fully grown gerbil is bigger than a mouse but smaller than a beaver. Show a picture of a gerbil or display a real one. An adult gerbil is about 4 inches long, with a tail also 4 inches long ($4 + 4 = 8$). Have the children cup their hands to show approximately 4 inches for the body, and keep their hands in the same position to show approximately 4 inches for the tail. (For contrast, cup hands to show a big horse and then cup hands to show its small tail—unequal parts.) You may do this for several animals, and then get back to the gerbil as having equal parts. Now have the children look around the room. How many equal parts can they find in the room? Examples are 3 windowpanes + 3 windowpanes; 2 big windows + 2 big windows; 1 sink handle + 1 sink handle; 5 lights + 5 lights. You might have the children draw the equations in rebus style. They can divide a sheet of paper in half and draw three windowpanes on the left side and three windowpanes on the right side, or two big windows on the left side and two big windows on the right side. This shows an equal number of items on each half of the paper.

Recipe for "Mousercizing." This activity is read and directed by you:

Let's pretend we are mice.
Crouch down low.
Nibble your cheese.
Wiggle your nose.
Squint your eyes.
Perk up your ears.

Turn your head to the left and look for the cat.
Turn your head to the right and look for the cat.

Stand up quietly.
Hold your arms up like paws.
Slowly walk around in a circle.
Sniff for the cat.
Sniff for the cheese.

"MEOW."
Jump out of the way!
Run in place ten times.
Turn and run in place ten more times.
The cat is gone. Whew!
You are safe.
Give a big sigh, AHHHHH.
Not too loud or the cat will hear you.
Give a quiet sigh, Ahhhhhh. (*encourage a whisper*)
Sit down and rest.

Quietly open the refrigerator door. (*from sitting position*)
Slowly, quietly, carefully reach for the cheese.
Twist, twist, twist off a little piece.
Shh! Shh! Slowly close the door.
Nibble the cheese.
Ummmmm, it's good. Pat your tummy.
Yawn silently and show your sharp teeth.
Put your head on your hand.
Squint your eyes.
Rest.

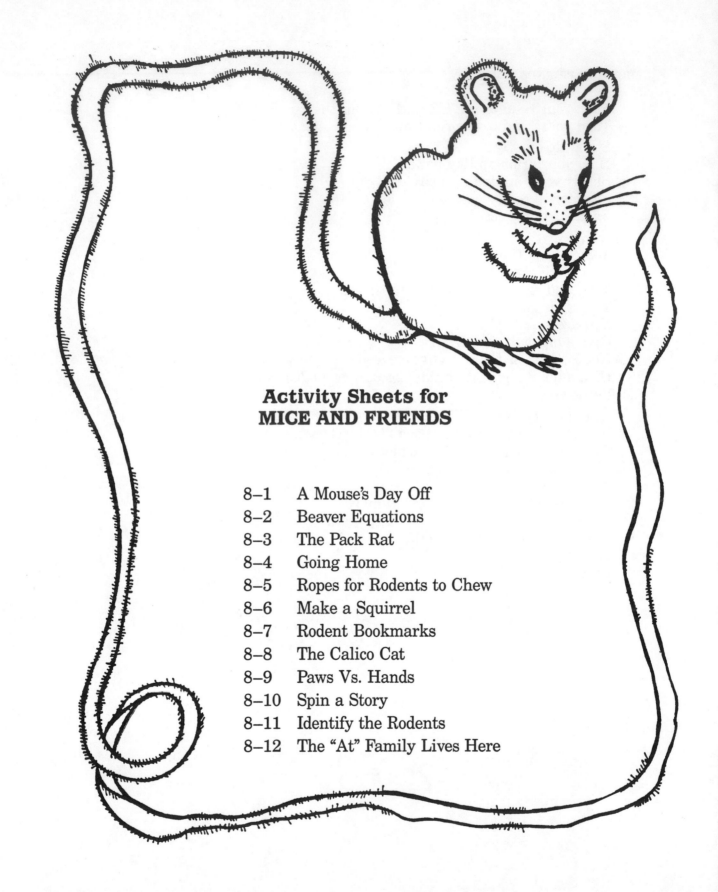

Activity Sheets for
MICE AND FRIENDS

Name

Date

A MOUSE'S DAY OFF

What does a mouse do on its day off? Write a creative story on the lines below, using the following words in your story: six, 5 o'clock, three. If you need more space, use the back of this sheet.

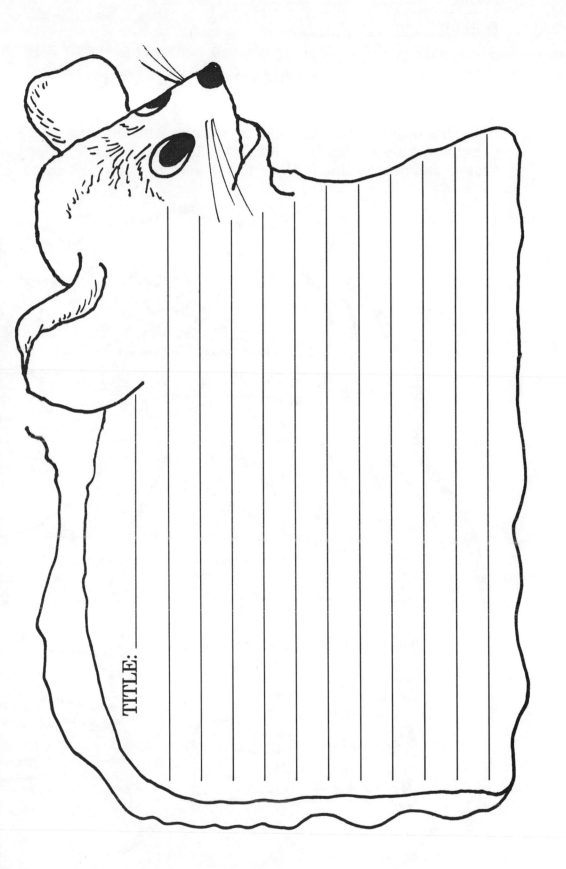

TITLE:

Name _____

Date _____

BEAVER EQUATIONS

Help this beaver build its home by making sure that the number sticks fit together. Complete the equation in Column A. The first one is done for you. Then look at the answer and draw a line to the number word in Column B that is the correct match.

A

7 + 3 = 10

6 + 3 = ___
4 + 2 = ___
3 + 4 = ___
2 + 6 = ___
3 + 2 = ___

B

Ten

six
seven
nine
five
eight

Name _____

Date _____

THE PACK RAT

This pack rat is a collector of things that shine. Look at the pictures at the bottom of this sheet and find the three things that shine. Cut out those squares and paste them in the pack rat's nest. Then color the rat a happy pink.

Name _____

Date _____

GOING HOME

A beaver must come up for air every five minutes. Trace this beaver's trail to its dam by connecting the dots and counting by five's. How many times must the beaver come up for air before reaching the dam? _____

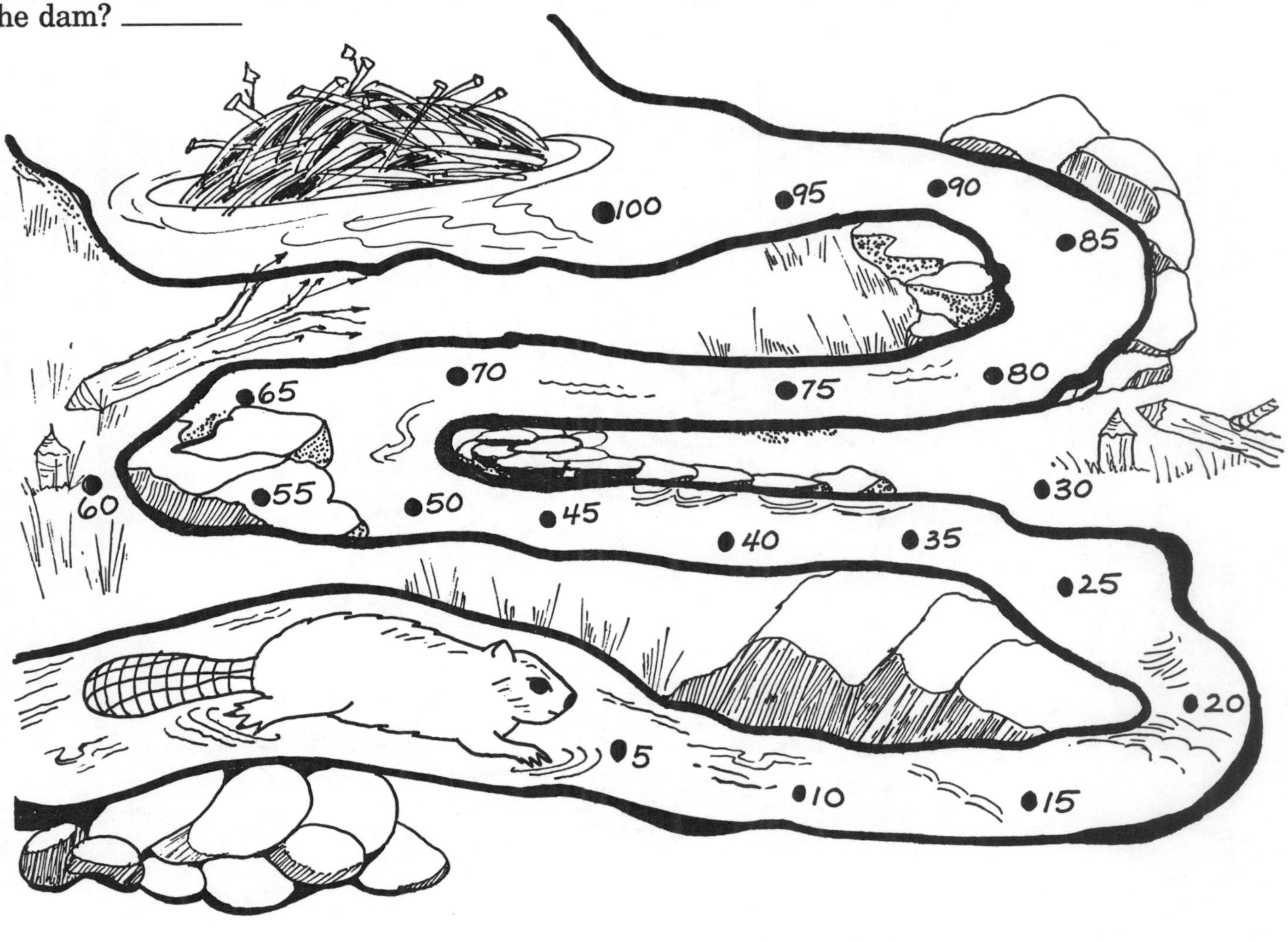

Name _____

Date _____

ROPES FOR RODENTS TO CHEW

How many inches of rope does each rodent have to chew? Using your ruler, measure each coil of rope from bottom to top and write the number of inches on the line below each coil. Then draw a rodent on top of the four other coils of rope.

5"

_____   _____   _____   _____

Name _____

Date _____

MAKE A SQUIRREL

Color this squirrel and its tail. Cut out the two pieces and fasten the tail to the body with a paper fastener. How would the squirrel use its tail in the wind, rain, snow, cold, and hot sun?

Name _____

Date _____

RODENT BOOKMARKS

Here are three bookmarks showing a prairie dog, a squirrel, and a beaver. Color each bookmark and write your name at the top of each one. Then cut each one out and write five facts about the particular rodent on the back of the bookmark. Use these bookmarks in your books as you read stories about these and other rodents.

Name _____

Date _____

THE CALICO CAT

Color this calico cat as it waits for a mouse. Color every number 1 white. Color every number 2 orange. Color every number 3 black. When you finish, turn this sheet over and draw a picture of a calico mouse.

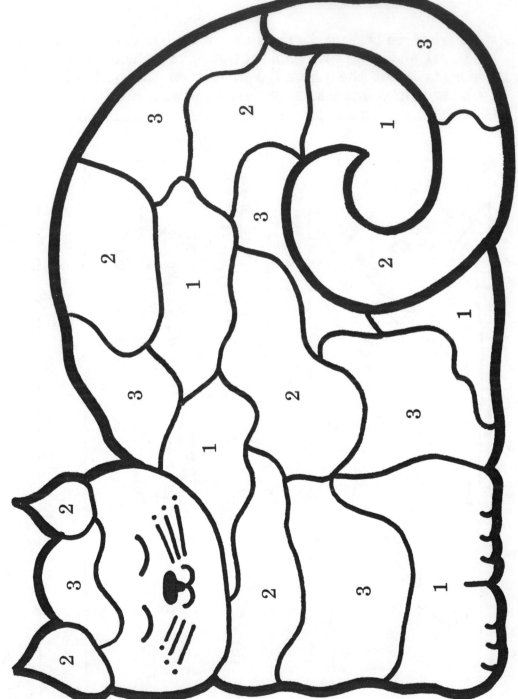

Name _____

Date _____

PAWS VS. HANDS

On the lines below, list five things a rodent can do with its paw. Then list five things you can do with your hands. Share your lists with your classmates.

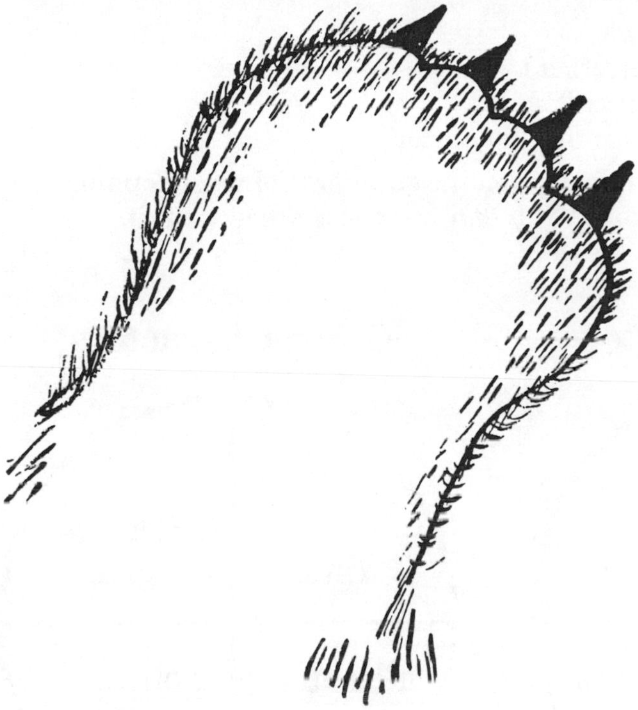

PAWS

_____

_____

_____

_____

_____

If you can think of more, write them on the back of this sheet.

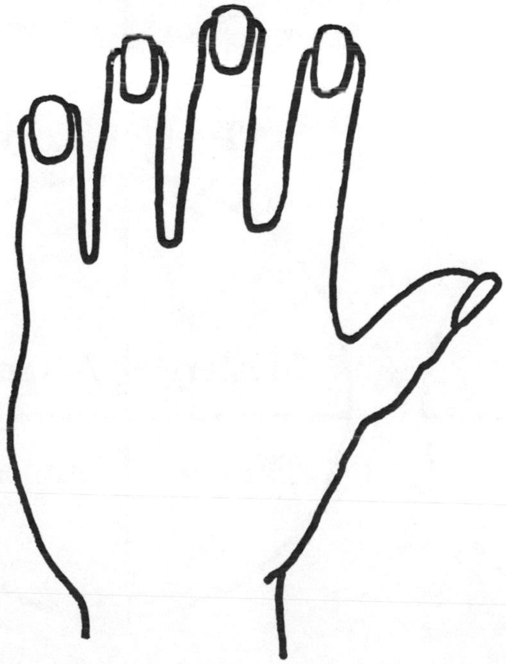

HANDS

_____

_____

_____

_____

_____

If you can think of more, write them on the back of this sheet.

Name _____

Date _____

SPIN A STORY

1. Cut out the four spinners at the bottom of this page.
2. Use a paper fastener to fasten one spinner to each circle.
3. Spin the spinner for each circle to determine

   Character (Who is the story about?)
   Other Characters (Makes good conversation.)
   Setting (Where does the story take place?)
   Type of story (How do you plan to entertain the reader?)

4. Now write your creative story using the information the spinners point to. You may illustrate your story if you wish. Remember, you can use these wheels again and again to create stories.

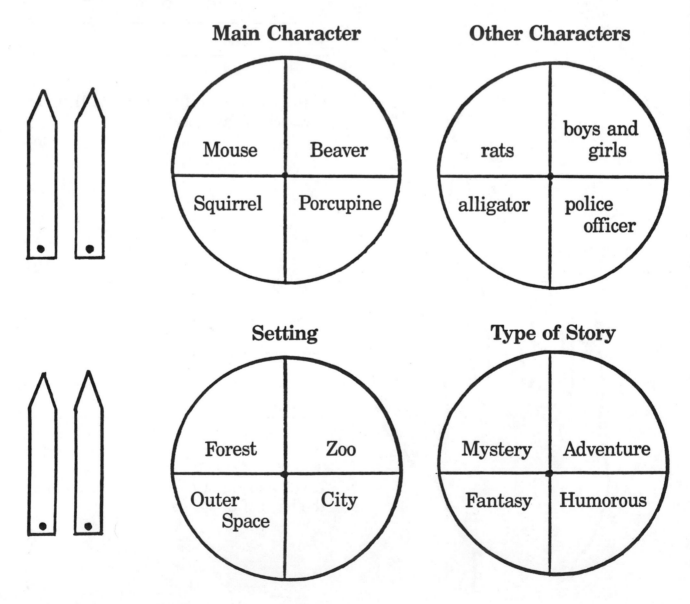

Main Character

Mouse | Beaver
Squirrel | Porcupine

Other Characters

rats | boys and girls
alligator | police officer

Setting

Forest | Zoo
Outer Space | City

Type of Story

Mystery | Adventure
Fantasy | Humorous

Name _____

Date _____

IDENTIFY THE RODENTS

Put an X on the two animals that are not rodents. Then draw a circle around the rodents and color them.

woodchuck

porcupine

bird

squirrel

rat

beaver

bear

chipmunk

prairie dog

Name _____

Date _____

THE "AT" FAMILY LIVES HERE

Look at the letters at the bottom of this sheet. Write each letter on a different line of the "at" sound and say that word to yourself. When the entire "At" family has moved in, draw a door and bushes or flowers in front to make the house look cheerful!

b   f   c   h   r   s   v   p   t   m

Section 9
UP, UP, AND AWAY!

Background Ideas and Other
Helpful Things to Know

Space travel is a great adventure that gives people the opportunity to explore the moon, the planets, and the stars. Giant rockets carry explorers, as well as weather satellites, communications satellites, navigation satellites, scientific satellites, and space probes into space.

Probably the main reason that people explore space is out of a longing to know. People have always been eager to explore the unknown. Scientists believe that space travel can answer many questions about the universe, such as how the sun, the planets, and the stars were formed, and whether there is life on other planets. As more powerful rockets are built, space travelers will be able to go to faraway planets and perhaps even to the stars.

The countdown for a space flight begins about 48 hours before T-zero or liftoff time. The astronauts don't arrive at the launch pad until a few hours before blastoff. They are well trained and in excellent physical condition. During the flight, they wear spacesuits that keep their bodies at a comfortable temperature. People in many different careers train to be astronauts.

There are many exciting careers in the space industry. The most exciting, of course, is exploring space as an astronaut. There are opportunities open to almost every kind of scientist and engineer, and to business administrators, doctors, and technicians. Information on space-age careers can be obtained from the following agencies: United States Office of Education, Division for Aerospace Education,

Washington, D.C. 20202; and American Institute of Aeronautics and Astronautics, 500 Fifth Avenue, New York, New York 10036.

Activity Suggestions

Who Would Be a Great Astronaut? Discuss with the children the qualities and capabilities that would be beneficial to anyone interested in being an astronaut. Ask them to write a story entitled either "I'd Be a Great Astronaut" or "I Nominate _____ to Be an Astronaut." The stories should describe *why* the person would be a good space traveler.

Homemade Spaceship. Call appliance stores in your area to locate a large empty appliance box (refrigerator size is good). With scissors, paint, and construction paper, turn the box into a spaceship, complete with pillows and a football helmet that the children can use as a space helmet. Have a tape recorder inside the ship so that the "astronauts" can describe what they see as they travel through the universe. You might also prepare a tape that gives instructions from back on Earth.

Aliens. Some scientists believe that there are other life forms on stars or planets in the universe. Have the children draw a picture of the space alien they would like to meet. Then have them write a story about the alien—what it likes to eat and think about, the kind of language it speaks, and what kinds of things it does every day.

Space aliens are creatures from other planets or stars. There are aliens in our country, too—people who are born in other countries of the world and come to live and work in America. Ask the children if any of them know people from other countries. How are these people like us and how are they different? Most of the ancestors of the children in the class were probably aliens when they came to America and were greeted by the Statue of Liberty. Have the children find out where their ancestors lived before coming to America.

Space Travel. Ask the students to write a story on "Where I would like to go if I could travel to any part of the universe." Ask why. Let the students share their stories in small groups.

Planets and Stars. Planets and stars look very much alike at night, but there are two ways to tell them apart. First, the planets shine with a steady light, while the stars seem to twinkle. Second, the planets change their position in relation to the stars. The ancient Greeks noticed this movement and called the moving objects *planetae*, meaning "wanderers." Have the children watch the night sky to see if they can distinguish between these two heavenly bodies.

Field Trip. If possible, visit a nearby planetarium with your students. Science museums will often have astronomy exhibits that can help the children learn about the solar system.

Constellations. Have the students research information about the constellations. They can recreate the star designs using dark blue construction paper and gummed silver and gold stars. Guide them in writing the names of the constellations on the blue paper with a white crayon.

Solar System Book. Together with the children, read Activity Sheets 9–10a and 9–10b. Guide the students in coloring the solar objects, cutting the pages apart on the lines, and stapling the sheets together in the proper order. The result is each child's very own book about the solar system.

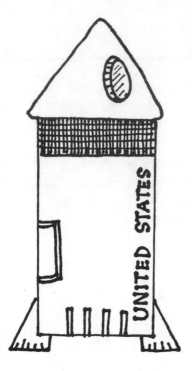

Activity Sheets for UP, UP, AND AWAY!

Name _____

Date _____

COUNTDOWN!

Whenever a rocket lifts off into space, there is a special countdown. Help this rocket lift off by writing the numbers from 10 down to 1 on the lines here. The 10 is written for you.

_____ 10 _____

_____

_____

_____

_____

_____

_____

_____

Blast off!

Name _____

Date _____

STARBRIGHT NUMBER SENTENCES

Draw a line from each number sentence on the left to the correct answer on the right.

Name _____ .

Date _____

COLOR THE ASTRONAUT

When Neil Armstrong became the first person to walk on the moon on July 20, 1969, he said, "That's one small step for a man, one giant leap for mankind." Read the special words here and then color the astronaut following this code: 1 = blue; 2 = red; 3 = yellow; 4 = orange; 5 = black.

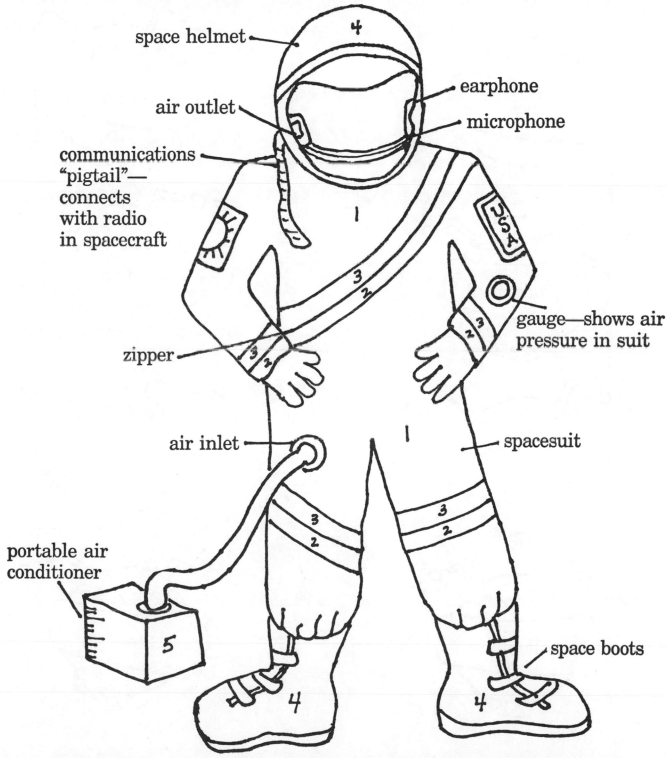

space helmet

earphone

microphone

air outlet

communications "pigtail"— connects with radio in spacecraft

gauge—shows air pressure in suit

zipper

air inlet

spacesuit

portable air conditioner

space boots

Name _____

Date _____

SATELLITE SOUNDS

These satellites are being sent into space to learn more about rhyming words. Draw a line from the satellite on the left to the correct rhyming word on the right. Say the words quietly to yourself.

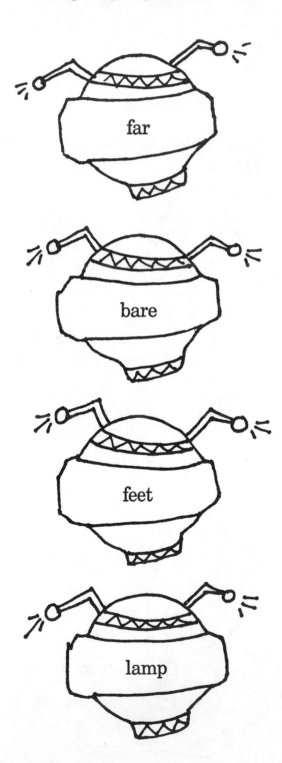

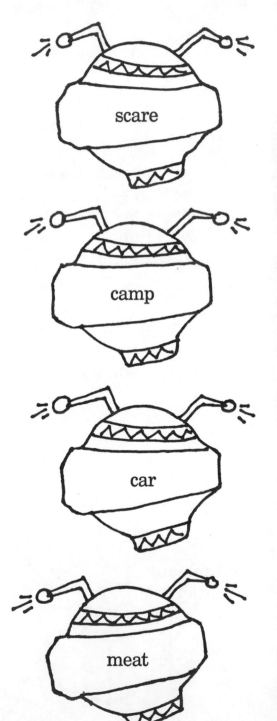

Name _____

Date _____

SUN SOUNDS

Each row of suns is a different word family. Fill in a different missing letter in each of the suns in the row to make a word. The first one in each row has been done for you. Be sure that each row has rhyming suns.

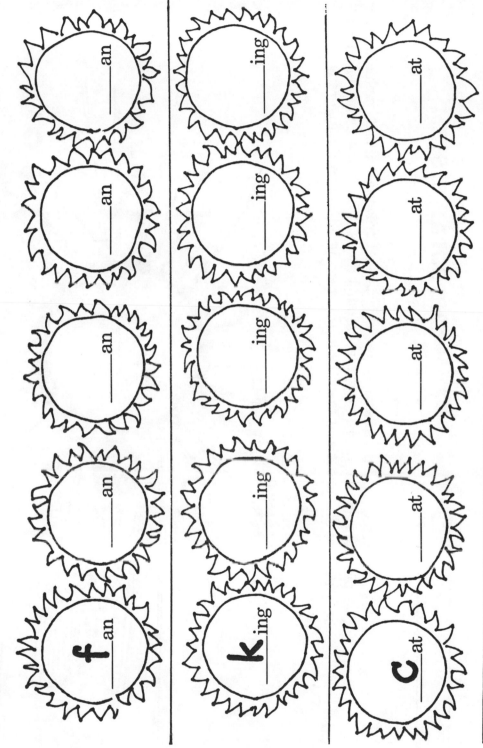

Name _____

Date _____

THE SOLAR SYSTEM

The solar system is the sun and all the objects that travel around it, including Earth and eight other planets and the moons that travel around them. Look at the names of some solar objects at the bottom of this sheet and then fill in the missing letters on the diagram.

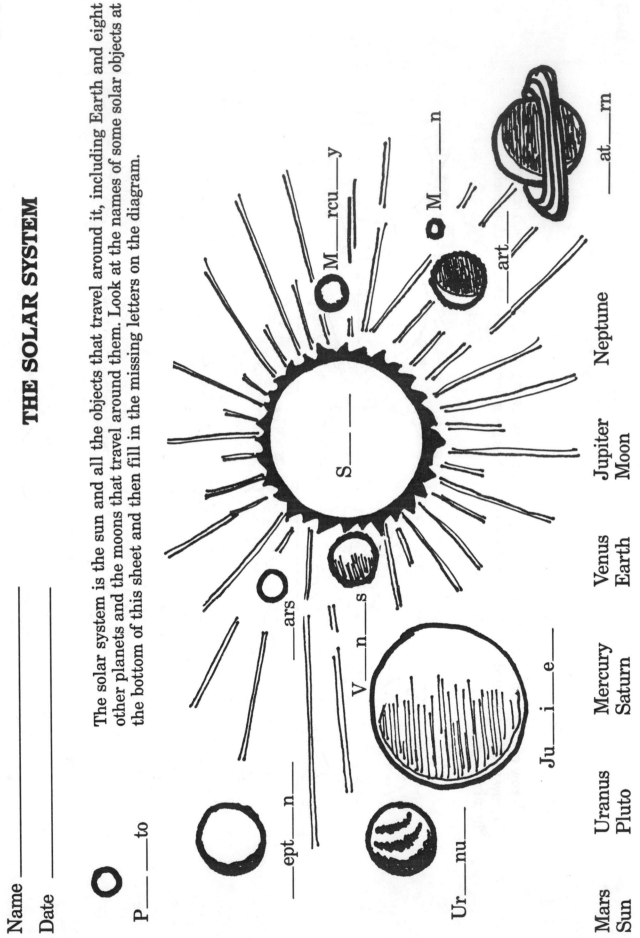

P___ to

ars

ept___n

Ur___nu___

Ju___i___e___

V___n___s

S___

M___rcu___y

M___n

art___

at___rn

Mars	Uranus	Mercury	Venus	Jupiter	Neptune
Sun	Pluto	Saturn	Earth	Moon	

Name _____

Date _____

"S" SPACE WORDS

Color these "S" space pictures and cut them out. Save them for the next activity sheet. Do you know what each picture is? Shown are sun, spaceship, Saturn, stars, satellite, and space traveler.

Name _____

Date _____

SPACE SCENE

Using the "S" word cutouts in activity 9–7, follow these directions: Paste the sun in the middle of this sheet. Paste the spaceship above the earth. Paste the space traveler to the right of the spaceship and draw a lifeline from the traveler to the ship. Paste Saturn in the lower right corner of the sheet. Paste the satellite in the lower left corner of the sheet. Paste the stars in the upper left part of the sheet.

X paste the spaceship here

X paste the traveler here

paste X stars here

X paste the sun here

X paste Saturn here

X paste the satellite here

Earth

Name _____

Date _____

MEASURE THE LAUNCH VEHICLES

A launch vehicle is a rocket or combination of rockets used to launch satellites, space probes, and other spacecraft. Use a ruler to measure each launch vehicle and write its height on the line.

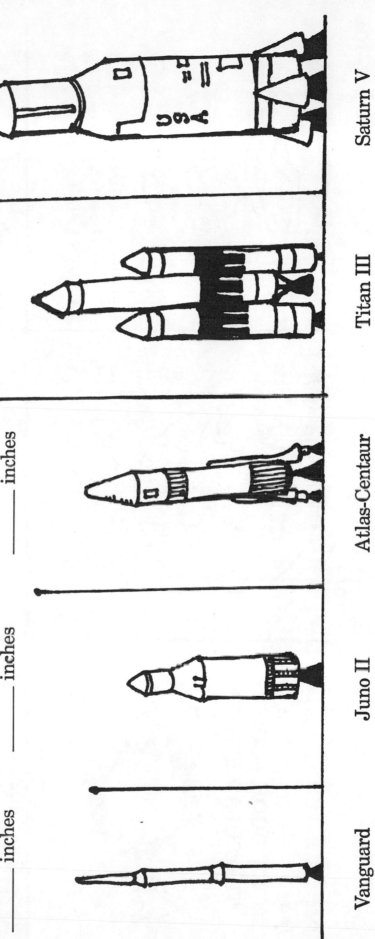

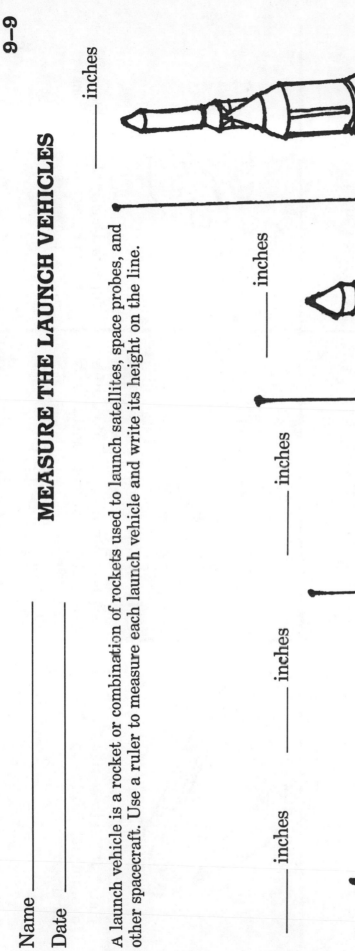

_____ inches

Saturn V

_____ inches

Titan III

_____ inches

Atlas-Centaur

_____ inches

Juno II

_____ inches

Vanguard

MY BOOK ABOUT
THE SOLAR SYSTEM

Name _____

1

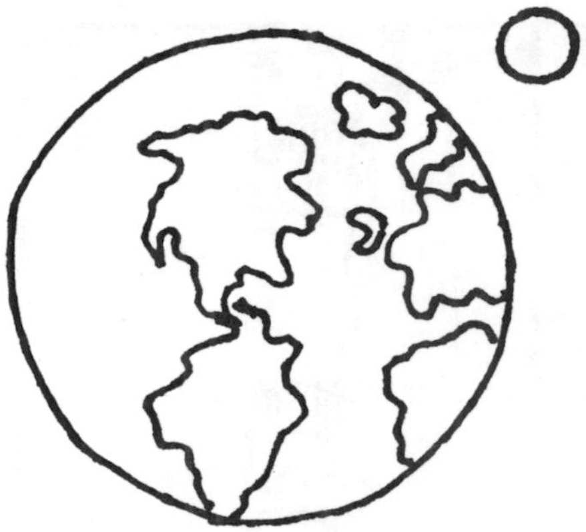

Earth is our planet. It has one satellite, or moon. The Earth is made mostly of iron and rock.

2

Jupiter is the largest planet. It is 30 times larger than Mercury, the smallest planet.

3

Saturn is the second largest planet. It has three thin flat rings around it, made up of tiny particles.

4

Pluto is the most distant planet from the sun. It cannot be seen without a telescope. Pluto travels around the sun once about every 248 years.

5

Mars is the only planet whose surface can be seen in detail from the Earth. It appears red.

6

Venus is called the Earth's "twin" because the two planets are similar in size. As seen from Earth, Venus is brighter than any other planet or star.

7

Uranus is the third farthest planet from the sun. Astronomers know almost nothing about the surface of the planet.

8

Neptune cannot be seen from Earth without a telescope. Scientists believe it is surrounded by clouds.

9

Mercury is the smallest planet and the one nearest the sun. It is dry, hot, and airless. Mercury goes around the sun once every 88 days.

10

The sun is the center of the solar system. The hugeness of the sun creates the gravitation that keeps the planets around the sun.

11

The stars are shining balls of hot gases. Nobody knows how many stars there are. Sometimes we see "falling stars" in the night sky. We make wishes on stars, too.

12

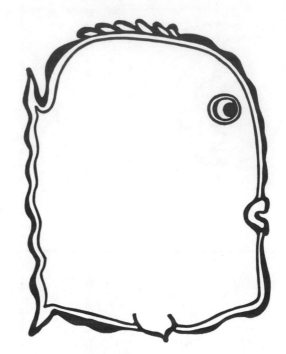

Section 10
SEA LIFE

Background Ideas and Other Helpful Things to Know

The salty oceans and seas are alive with fish, snakes, huge turtles, and sea mammals such as whales, dolphins, seals, and walrus.

Mammals differ from fish in that they give birth to their young, instead of laying eggs. Also, mammals have lungs and must surface for air. Their body temperature does not change with the water temperature. On the other hand, fish are cold-blooded. If a fish swims in cold water, its temperature is lowered; if it swims in warm water, its temperature rises. A fish is very much at home in the water and does not need to surface for air.

People are fascinated by sea creatures, particularly by the dolphin (a toothed whale). The dolphin is intelligent, playful, easily trained, and has a highly developed sonar communication system. Other whales have been trained in captivity, and some scientists believe that this is possible because these whales are fed regularly, and are not continually on the hunt for food.

Oceanographers, people who study sea life, have some sophisticated methods of tracking pathways and patterns of fish and mammals. Sometimes this is done by sound tracking. People are learning more and more about the migration routes of sea life and their habits in the water.

Activity Suggestions

The Baleen Whale. There are two types of whales—the toothed whale and the baleen whale. Although the baleen whale does not have teeth, it does have fringes (just like long stiff strings) that hang from the gums of the upper jaw. This substance is called "baleen" and consists mainly of keratin, which is much like our fingernails. When the baleen whale swims with its mouth open, small sea creatures floating in the water become tangled in the baleen. When the whale closes its mouth, the food that is trapped gets pushed down the throat with the tongue. Perhaps that's why we so often see pictures of whales with their jaws open—they're fishing for food.

To reinforce the concept of the baleen, have the children examine their fingernails closely. Notice that although they are hard, they are pliable or flexible. Ask: How do our fingernails help us? (They are useful in picking up objects, for scraping, as protection for the top of our fingers, and so on.)

Baleen is sometimes called "whalebone," although it is not bone. Among other things, it has been used as a tool (needle) and has been used as the rib portion of umbrellas. The size and shape of baleen varies from one type of whale to another. For example, the baleen of the gray whale is 18 inches long and the baleen of the bowhead whale is 14 feet long. Measure these variations using the yardstick, and just imagine the size of those jaws!

Set up a Whale Study Area in the classroom where the children can become "trapped' (fascinated) as they enter the area to read, study, and write about whales.

The Toothed Whale. Toothed whales range in size from 5-foot dolphins to 54-foot great sperm whales. Use a trundle wheel to measure the imaginary pink dolphin in the corridor and the polka-dot sperm whale on the playground. Measure and cut string to make the comparison.

The toothed whale uses its teeth to catch fish and squid, but it does not chew the food; rather, it swallows the food whole. The teeth are used for catching and hanging onto the food—like carrying your very own built-in set of fishing equipment. The toothed whale is always prepared for the catch!

Teeth are important to the dolphin in the same way for catching food but not for chewing. However, teeth are very important to people for eating food (biting, chewing, grinding) but usually not for catching food. Thus, teeth are important to both dolphins and people, but for different reasons. Have a large mirror available at eye level so that the children can show and see their teeth. Have them count their uppers and lowers using only their tongue. The children can learn and review the names of teeth (incisors, bicuspids, and cuspids). Ask: What is the function of each? What do the names mean?

This is also a good time to begin a "brushing campaign" and remember that the teeth are brushed up and down. When was the last time the children got a new toothbrush? What color is it? How often do they use it? What is flossing? Some dentists feel that flossing is as important as brushing.

Using the chalkboard, draw giant teeth along the top and bottom edges. Using a long-handled brush or broom and some water, let the children take turns brushing up and down. This is a good exercise for large muscle development and eye-hand coordination (or visual-motor integration).

Krill. Also known as water shrimp, krill is the favorite food of the baleen whale. Water shrimp are just a little more than one inch in length and bright red in color. They live near the surface of the water. At times, there are so many krill traveling together that they take up an area the size of a football field (100 yards from goal to goal). Whales may eat as much as three tons of krill each day. This is a difficult concept for youngsters to understand, but to give them the idea that it is a tremendous weight, bring in a 5-pound bag and a 10-pound bag of potatoes, and let the children take turns lifting the weights.

Then say that if krill could be purchased in 5-pound bags, it would take 1,200 bags to feed the whale. If krill could be purchased in 10-pound bags, it would take 600 bags to feed the whale. And that's just for one day! Is it any wonder, then, that some whales have been referred to as the "wolves of the sea" (since wolves are perceived as being perpetually hungry)?

The Killer Whale. This is the real "sea wolf" and is enemy to all other whales. The killer whale, hunting in packs of 30 to 40 much like wolf packs on land, can travel up to 25 miles per hour as it speeds through the water. How fast does a goldfish travel in one minute, and how far? Let the children time and measure this.

The Friendly Dolphin. Have children help measure and make a 5-foot long gray construction paper dolphin for the bulletin board. You can double the paper, staple the edges, and stuff it. (The children can pretend to be feeding fish to the dolphin as they insert paper scraps to fill out the shape.) Ask the children to propose three different names for the dolphin and then vote on the name that they like best. Now your dolphin has become a member of the class.

Since training a dolphin requires "drill and practice," make sets of math facts, spelling words, sea creature information, and so on, on paper fish. Place the sets inside of nets made from used onion or potato bags and have the children try to answer the cards. The number correct is the number of "fish" the children can "feed" to the dolphin. Keep track daily of the number of fish fed to the dolphin.

A variation to this activity is "Beat the Dolphin." The dolphin already knows all of the answers, which you have written on the reverse side of the fish. With very young children, this can be done with the total group; older children may want to work alone or with a partner. Keep score daily.

Crocodilians. When scientists use the term "crocodilians," they are referring to alligators and crocodiles, which are reptiles with long tails and snouts, sharp teeth, tough skin, and four short fat legs. They spend part of their time in water and part on land, and can grow to be 15 to 20 feet in length.

How can you tell alligators from crocodiles? When a crocodile's mouth is closed, you can still see its teeth, especially the bottom ones. When an alligator's mouth is closed, you usually won't see teeth, especially the bottom ones. Also, the crocodile has a round nose, while the alligator's is pointed.

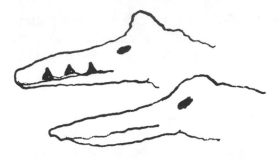

Use crocodiles and alligators when teaching the concept of opposites. Tell the children that if the crocodile (a paper cutout showing teeth) owns all of the round items in class and the alligator (a paper cutout showing no teeth) owns all of the square items, then let's make a list of what each one owns. This can also be done with the concepts of up and down, big and little, over and under, cold and hot, and so on.

The Sea Turtle. Five kinds of sea turtles live in the ocean: Leatherback, Loggerhead, Green, Ridley, and Hawksbill. Let the children get books from the library and find pictures of each type of turtle. What are the similarities and differences? Which are endangered species? Guide the students in cutting out large construction paper turtles in order to write their reports, or information, on the shell portion.

Visit a Sandy Beach. Many sea animals live at the water's edge. At low tide, sea creatures are buried in the sand and at high tide they live in the water—but they *always* have to be wet. If you live near a sandy shore, bring the children to dig to find sand dollars, clams, starfish, sea urchins, and snails. If this is not possible, show picture books to identify these seashore creatures. If someone has a shell collection to share with the class, display the items in a big bucket of sand.

Waterproof Creatures. Sea creatures have waterproof skin, meaning that water cannot seep through. Explain that many items we use are waterproof. Together with the children, make a list of these items (plastic umbrella, slicker, rubber boots, raincoat, special underwater watch and camera, and so on) and how they help us.

Sea Creature Book. Make a "Meet the Sea Creatures" book. Have the students include on each page the name of the sea creature, the weight, length, and diet, as well as other information they can find. Encourage the children to draw pictures of the creatures and then prepare a book cut in the shape of one of the creatures. Library reference books could be used so that there is a variety of sea creatures, such as the sea otter (smallest mammal with a thick coat of fur), the manatee (big and gentle and called the "sea cow"), seals (elephant seals are the biggest), and the walrus (tusks begin to grow at the age of two years).

An Abundance of Fish. Some names for fish are jellyfish, grouper, mackerel, herring, tuna, cod, halibut, haddock, perch, and spot. There are many, many more. Ask the children to find out what kinds are abundant in their area and in their state.

Sink or Float. An object floats by taking up an amount of water equal to its weight, a process called "displacement." Set up an area that has a plastic tub half filled with water and a tray of items for the students to place in the water one at a time to see whether the item will sink or float. Let older children record the results of their investigation.

Fossils. Some fossils are bones or shells that have turned to stone over thousands of years. Explain that fossils of sea and plant animals have even been found on mountains. What is a common fossil found in your area? If you do not have real fossils for the children to see, encourage them to visit the local museum or arrange for a field trip. Contact the high school science department to see if specimens can be loaned or invite a collector to class.

Let the children make "fake fossils." Using a flattened piece of plasticene as the base, press a shell down into it and then gently remove the shell. The indentations of several varieties of shells on the clay give the appearance of a fossilized sample.

A School of Fish. Many fish travel together in groups, called a "school of fish." If there were actually a school *for* fish, list (with the children) the things the fish would have to learn in swim class, water safety class, driving class, and so on.

We're All Wet (Almost). More than 70 percent of the earth is underwater. Show this to the children using a globe and a large wall map, and demonstrate by percent wheels what this concept means. (Seven of the ten parts, or 70 percent, of the circle should be colored in.) Work on other percentages using the percent wheel. (See Activity Sheet 10–11 for other percent wheels.)

Using Your Antennae and Feelers. Many sea creatures must find their way about by feeling. Have the children work in pairs and take turns being a sea creature that cannot see (use a blindfold). Let them feel objects (rough seashell, smooth seashell, sponge, sea horse, starfish, pebble, and so on) that have been placed inside a bag and identify them by touch.

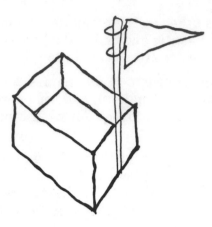

A Box Boat. You need a large box, dowel rod, cloth sail, and string. Optional materials are goggles, fins, lifejacket, inner tube, and telescope. For creative play, have one or two children get into the box boat and "sail away." When they return, ask them to draw a picture of two things they saw during their voyage.

Activity Sheets for
SEA LIFE

Name _____

Date _____

COLOR ME GORGEOUS!

Many fish are beautifully colored with spots and stripes. Become a fashion designer and make this fish look stunning.

Make a fancy fish puppet from a colorful old sock. Glue on scrap materials (velvet, satin, lace, chintz, ruffles, and so on). Wear your fish and have it dive, glide, do flips, and even "swim" to music!

Name

Date

DESIGNER SEA GOGGLES

Cut out the goggles below and glue a different color of cellophane (yellow, blue, and green) on the back of each. Use the goggles for creating a mood when listening to a sea story or while painting a picture. Also use them to examine seashells and coral. Remember that the sea gets increasingly darker the farther down you go.

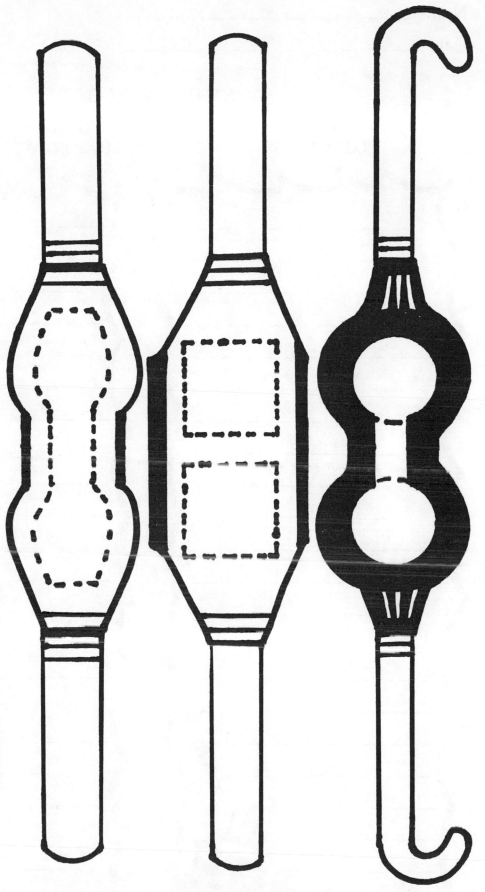

Name _____

Date _____

SINK OR FLOAT

THINGS THAT SINK

THINGS THAT FLOAT

Name _____

Date _____

WHICH ONE IS DIFFERENT?

In each row, find the one that is different and put an X on it. Then color the two in that row which are the same.

Name _____

Date _____

THE PIRATE'S SECRET CODE

1. On another sheet of paper, write ten names of sea creatures using this code. Exchange papers with a partner to decipher the names.
2. Write a sea story on another sheet of paper. Use the code for every tenth word.
3. Make a treasure map on a large sheet of paper. Use the code to disguise the names of places and things.

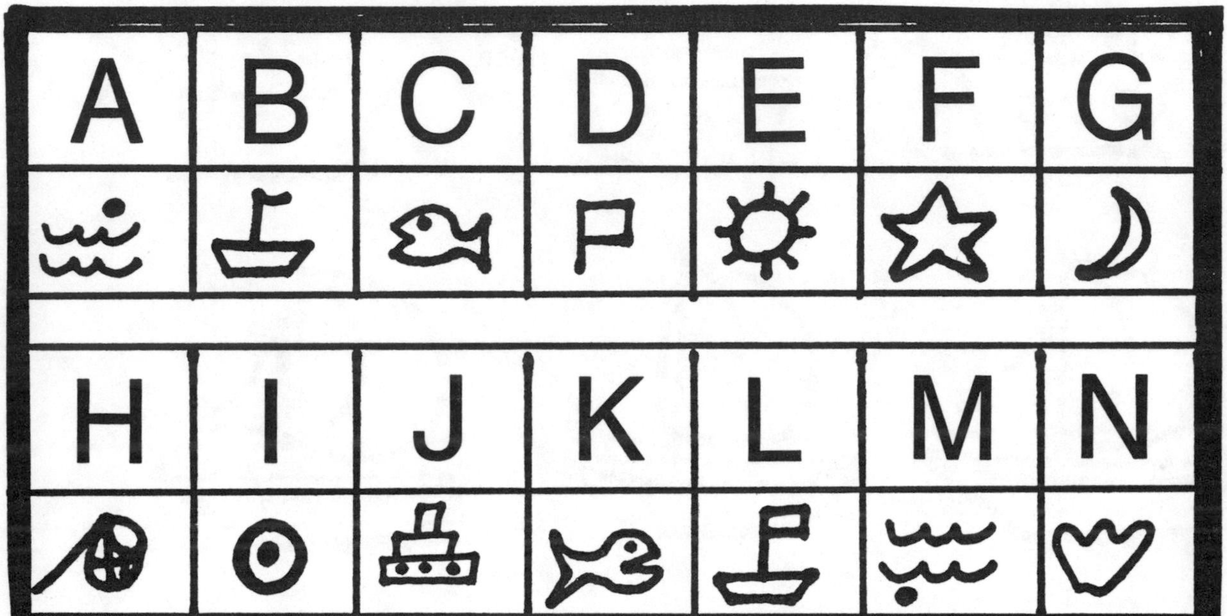

Name _____

Date _____

MATCH THE SEASHELLS

Color these shells and then draw a line from each shell on the left to its twin on the right. The first one is done for you. Can you identify these seashells?

Name _____

Date _____

CROCODILIAN MENU

Here's your chance to create a menu for alligators and crocodiles, who like to eat tadpoles, small fish, frogs, turtles, snails, and bugs. Crocodiles also eat stones and pebbles to help grind their food. Be sure to make appetizing names for your soups, sauces, and main dishes!

Appetizer

Special of the Day

Main Dish

Dessert

Beverage

Name _____

Date _____

CONDUCT A WEIGHT SURVEY

A whale can weigh 2 tons (4,000 pounds) at birth! Find out how many pounds you weighed when you were born. Then color in the rectangle above that numeral in this chart. Put your initials on the rectangle, too. One by one, ask other people the same question. Color the rectangles and put their initials on the chart, too. You are conducting a survey.

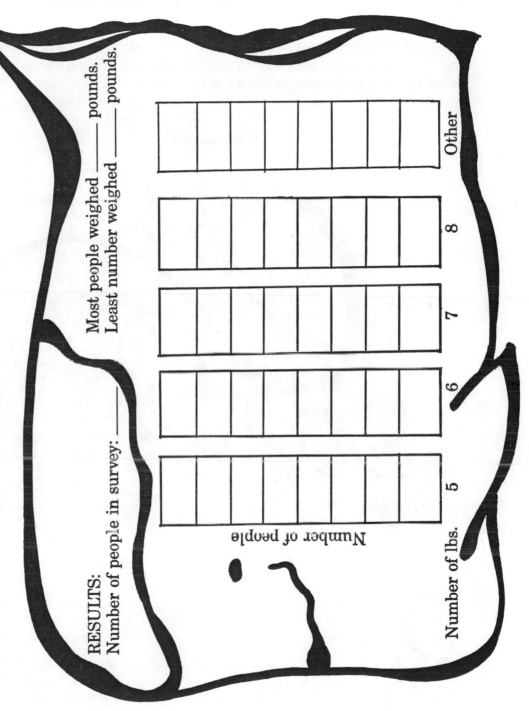

RESULTS:

Number of people in survey: _____

Most people weighed _____ pounds.

Least number weighed _____ pounds.

Number of people

Number of lbs.   5   6   7   8   Other

Name _____

Date _____

RIDE A DOLPHIN!

Congratulations! You have the winning ticket for a ride on a friendly dolphin. Describe the sights, sounds, and colors you experience during your ride. Use the back of this sheet if you need more space to write.

SPOUTING WITH
GOOD NEWS ABOUT WHALES

Name _____

Date _____

Write some interesting facts about whales on the lines below.

Name _____

Date _____

PERCENT WHEELS

Help this sea mammal balance the percent wheels.
Color in the correct portion of each circle.

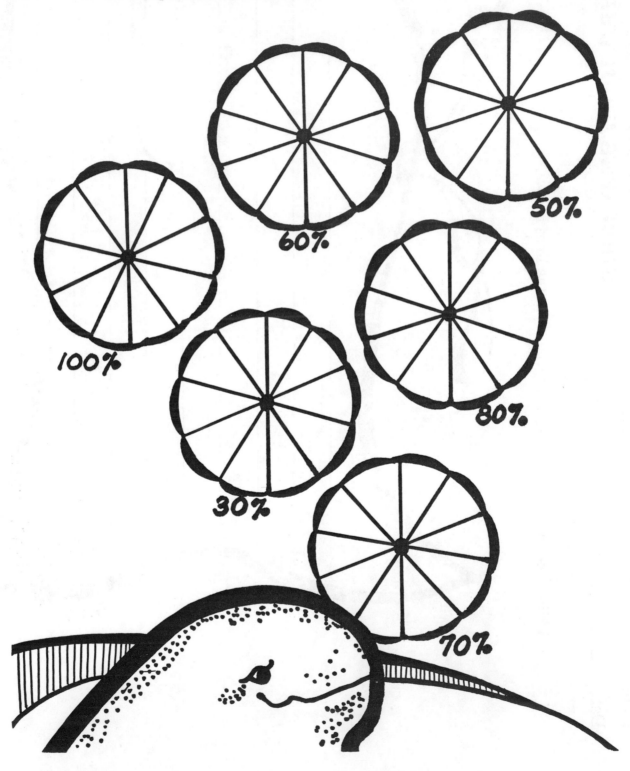

Name _____

Date _____

BURIED TREASURE

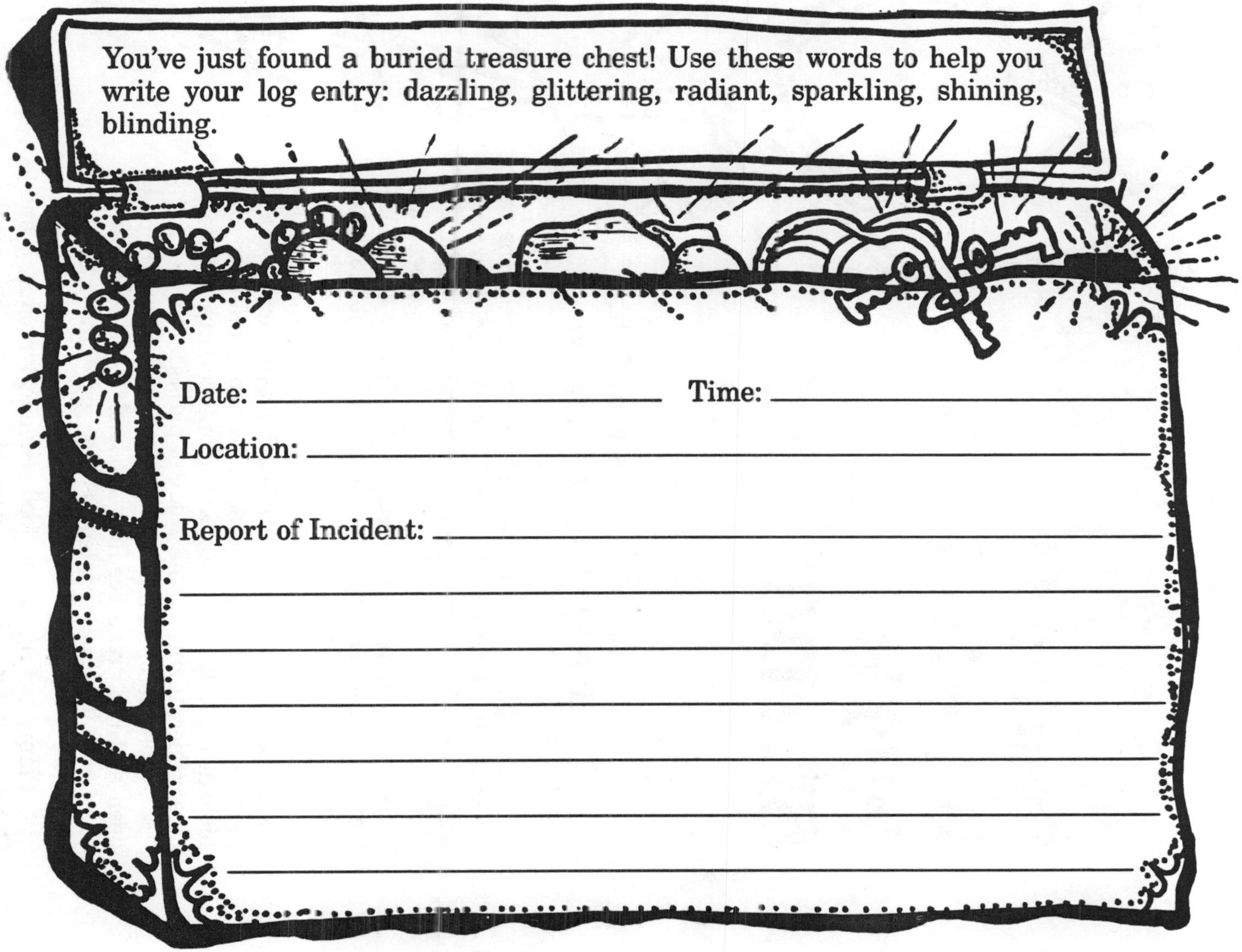

You've just found a buried treasure chest! Use these words to help you write your log entry: dazzling, glittering, radiant, sparkling, shining, blinding.

Date: _____

Time: _____

Location: _____

Report of Incident: _____

Section 11
BURSTING WITH SEEDS

Background Ideas and Other Helpful Things to Know

Every plant, from the very simplest one-celled bacteria to the largest living tree, can be classified. There are well over 350,000 plants that exist in the world, so classification is essential. Latin is the language used for classifying plants because scientists all over the world can use it and be sure they are talking about the same thing.

"Ecology" refers to our environment, so plant ecologists study the way plants are affected by their surroundings (water, sunlight, and soil). "Botany" refers to the biological study of plants, and plant botanists make a career specializing in the study of plants.

A seed becomes a plant when the seed coating bursts open and the green seedling is visible. The seedling (a plant with less than five leaves) then grows into a mature plant.

Plants are used for food, chemical products, and fibers, and are also a source of pleasure for people because of their variety of beautiful colors, fragrances, and shapes.

Activity Suggestions

Perennials and Annuals. There are perennial flowers and annual flowers. Write the terms on the chalkboard. Make sure that the children understand that perennial flowers reseed themselves and come up year after year (iris, tulip, chrysanthemum), whereas annual flower seeds have to be planted each year (petunia, zinnia).

What's Inside a Seed? A tiny plant is inside each fertile seed. Plant a variety of seeds in styrofoam cups. Encourage the children to make some predictions, such as: Which seeds will germinate (sprout) first? How long will it take? When seedlings appear, how many inches will they grow in one week? Let the students keep a record of this.

Apple   Bean   Pea   Orange   Pansy   Marigold

In order to show explicitly what is inside a seed, conduct the following experiment. You need a glass jar, blotter or paper towel, lima beans, and water. *Directions:* Encircle the inside of the jar with a piece of blotter or toweling. Wet the toweling and place one inch of water in the bottom of the container—just enough to be touching the toweling so that it can soak up the water and keep wet. Then place the seeds between the blotter and jar. The seeds will sprout within a couple of days, a process the children can actually observe through the glass. They will see the seed cover opening and the growth of seedlings and roots. These plants can then be planted in dirt (and the children *know* the roots are there). Measure the plant growth daily using a ruler and keep a growth record on a nearby chart.

Estimation of Sunflower Seeds. Get a large can with a lid and fill it with sunflower seeds, which can be purchased at a garden store. Have each child estimate the number of seeds inside the container. Spill them out and let the students sift through them with their hands. Take ten seeds from the pile and isolate them to give children a point of reference from which to make a thoughtful comparison. Use a "Sign Up Sheet" to record each child's name and his or her estimate. When everyone has made an estimation, count the seeds.

Keep the container of seeds in a handy spot so that the children can use the seeds to count to 100 by making piles of ten, five, and two. Point out that the groups containing the larger numbers can be more easily and quickly counted.

Another activity is to plant some sunflower seeds both indoors and outdoors. Tell the children that some sunflowers grow over ten feet tall. How high is ten feet? fifteen feet? twenty feet? If at all possible, give the students the experience of seeing and touching a real giant sunflower that is filled in the center with the large, bumpy seeds. Look at the radial patterning of the sunflower seeds. Can the children think of any other items in nature that have radial patterns?

Compare Yourself to a Giant Beanstalk. Construct a giant stem from green construction paper and tape it on the wall or on the side of a cupboard so that it extends from floor to ceiling. Have each child stand against the stem sheet while you mark his or her height in inches and label the mark with the child's name. Make height comparisons using such terms as "taller than" and "shorter than." Be sure to measure yourself, principal, and guests. You can also make a "Class Height Bar Graph" using fractions of inches.

Seed Classification in a Muffin Tin. Have the students collect seeds and bring them to school. Encourage the children to come up with ways to classify the seeds (by size, shape, texture, color) in a large muffin tin. The children can save seeds from lunch items (apples, oranges, grapefruits, plums, peaches), wash and dry the seeds, and add them to the collection.

Vocabulary Books. Fold and staple together five sheets of 4-by-6-inch paper with a construction paper cover. Decorate the cover and make up a catchy title, such as "Plant Talk." Have the children decide on a vocabulary word to print on each side (this could be a "word-a-day"). Guide the students in looking up the meaning of the word and writing it in the book. Ask the children to use the word in a sentence and draw a picture illustrating the word. Some possible words to include are: stem, leaf, flower, bud, root, embryo, seeds, photosynthesis, chlorophyl, cotyledon, sepals, stamen, pistil, petals, and pollinate.

Seeds Are Stored Food. Rather than plant seeds in the ground, tell the children that we can eat some of them. For example, bread, muffins, and cakes are made from wheat and corn that have been ground or mashed to make flour or meal. Let the children experience grinding or mashing seeds into meal. Encourage them to sing "Jimmy Crack Corn" as they work rhythmically to grind or mash seeds.

Make bread, cookies, cakes, or muffins with the students. This is a splendid opportunity to give children experience with liquid and dry measure. Try to make something "from scratch" rather than from mixes, and let the children sprinkle poppy seeds or sesame seeds on top of their food. Enlist the aid of the kitchen staff to help with the baking *or* select a recipe that can be used with a crockpot in the classroom. Time and its importance in cooking and baking food can be another focus of this activity.

For a snack, cut a variety of bread slices (stone-ground wheat, whole wheat, rye, and so on) into four squares (good for fractions). Spread the bread (or crackers) with honey and sprinkle with chopped nuts (like the peanut, which is a seed).

Ask parents to send in favorite recipes using seeds (rice, corn, wheat, and so on). Compile the recipes and make a class "Seed Recipe Book." Here you can expand your seed menu to include things like rice pudding, corn relish, and cereals.

Create a cooking experience chart with the class. Have the children tell you, in order, all of the things that you did (procedure) to prepare a food. This activity strengthens sequential thinking and recall. Children can make rebus drawings on the chart, too.

Plants Absorb Water. You need a knife, three containers of water, three celery stalks, and three different food colorings (red, blue, yellow).

Directions: Half fill each container with water, and add a different food coloring to each one. Cut one inch from the bottom of each celery stalk and gently spread the fibers, which allows for quicker absorption. Place one celery stalk in each container. Notice how the colored water disperses through the stem, showing the veins and pathways for absorbing the water. Does one color show the pathway better than another? Which one? Have the children examine the stalks with a magnifying glass and draw the results. On another day, place cross sections of the celery stalks under a microscope and let the children draw their observations. (See Activity Sheet 11–2.)

State Flowers. Make a large map of the country and ask the students if they know that each state has a flower (symbol). Make a list of each state and guide the children to find out the state flower and draw a picture of the flower on the map. Here are some state flowers to help you get started: New Jersey—violet; Ohio—red carnation; Tennessee—iris; California—golden poppy; Florida—orange blossom; New York—wild rose; Kansas—sunflower. How many are perennials and how many are annuals? Does your community have a flower? Does the classroom have a flower? Does each child have a favorite flower?

Plants That Heal. Some plants have provided the answers to diseases of humans and some are poisonous to people. Discuss the benefits from plants (strophanthus vine—coritsone; mold—penicillin; citrus—vitamin C). The aloe plant appears on the pharmacy shelf in a variety of products. Try to bring in an aloe plant (available from a florist or garden store) and break one of the spiny stalks to show the clear liquid within. When used externally on the skin, it has proved useful, especially for burns.

Get two jars and make colorful paper labels for them. On small pieces of paper, print the names of beneficial plants and poisonous plants. See if the children can classify them accurately.

Plant an Herb Garden. Make your own herb garden using such well-known seeds as basil, marjoram, parsley, sage, rosemary, thyme, winter savory, and dill. Do some library research to find out the use of herbs as a remedy (open sores, sore throats, stomach aches, toothaches) and for flavoring foods (soups, salads, stews). Be sure to caution the children not to eat growing things that they find outdoors unless they check with an adult and are absolutely sure that the plant is harmless.

A variation to this activity is to plant herb seeds in styrofoam cups so that each student has one. Once the herb has sprouted, send it home to flourish on sunny kitchen windowsills. An accompanying recipe using this herb will be a great way to inform parents of this section on seeds.

Perhaps an herb-grower in the community can be invited to address the class on the benefits and uses of herbs. Check with your local historical society or a nearby garden nursery. (See Activity Sheet 11–11.)

Musical Instruments. You need heavy-duty small paper plates, a variety of seeds (rice, nuts, peas), glue, and markers. *Directions:* Place several seeds on different paper plates. Place other paper plates upside down on each plate with seeds and glue the edges together. When thoroughly dry, use markers to decorate the plates with colorful designs. Then each day, encourage a "Seed Rhythm Band" to shake the plates in time to music.

Traveling Seeds in a Bag. For the Science Table, bring in milkweed pods and place them inside a large plastic bag. Then, when the pods burst open, the seeds won't travel all over the room but are captured inside a see-through bag for investigation. Do the same with cattails and dandelions.

The Medicine Man and the Space-Age Medicine Person. Currently, drug researchers are examining tiny black dots (particles) that have been brought back to Earth from outer space by astronauts. No one knows what the future will bring in the way of cures for diseases. Encourage the children to create stories about how the world might be a healthier, better place to live because of using some of these tiny dots in medicine.

In the past, ceremonial masks were worn by the medicine man of a tribe. This person knew just the right herbs, plants, and chants to effect cures. Encourage the children to create chants, such as:

Boom Bah! Boom Bah!

Ha! Ha! Ha!

Moo-may! Moo-may!

La! La! La!

How would a medicine man from the past and a space-age medicine person communicate? (Use the masks from Activity Sheets 11–4 and 11–5 for creative play.)

As a variation of this activity, have the children invent three-dimensional health "machines," such as an X-ray machine, dentist drill and equipment, stethoscope, and so on. Help the children use inexpensive or disposable items (aluminum foil, various sized boxes, paper towel rolls, empty food cans, styrofoam packing, silver and gold spray paint, and so on) to construct these health aids.

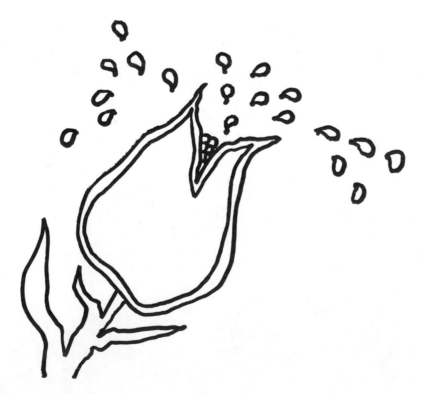

Activity Sheets for
BURSTING WITH SEEDS

Name _____

Date _____

A GOOD HARVEST

We had a good harvest this year because every seed sprouted! Draw a line from the number of seeds on the left to the correct number of food items on the right. The first one is done for you.

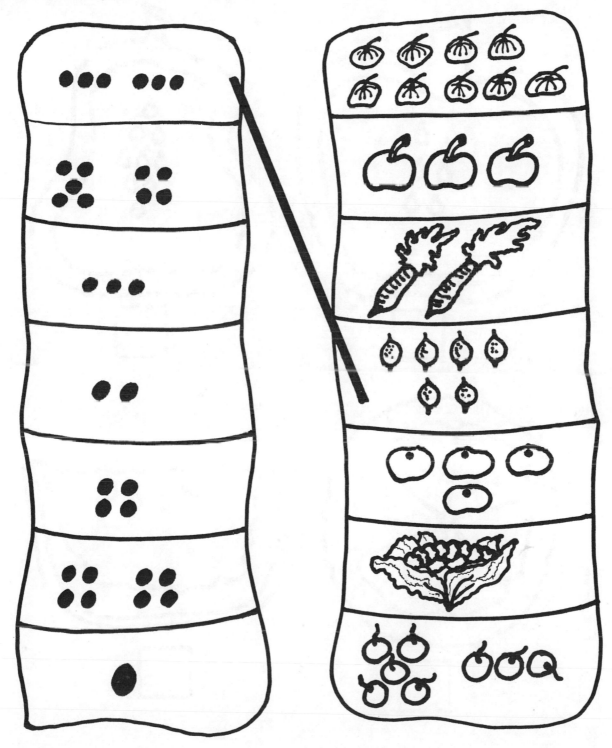

Name _____

Date _____

HOW MANY SEEDS?

Count the seeds in each piece of fruit and write the numeral in the box below each fruit. When you're finished, color the fruit.

PUT THEM IN ORDER

Color these four pictures and cut out each one. Then use the four pictures on Activity Sheet 11–4 by pasting them in sequential order on the boxes.

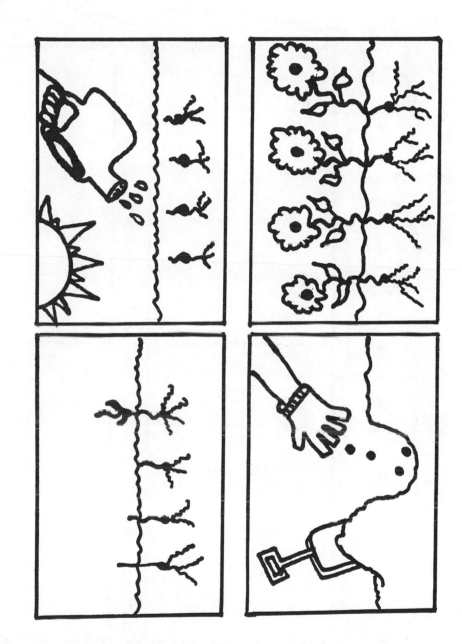

Name _____

Date _____

MY GARDEN

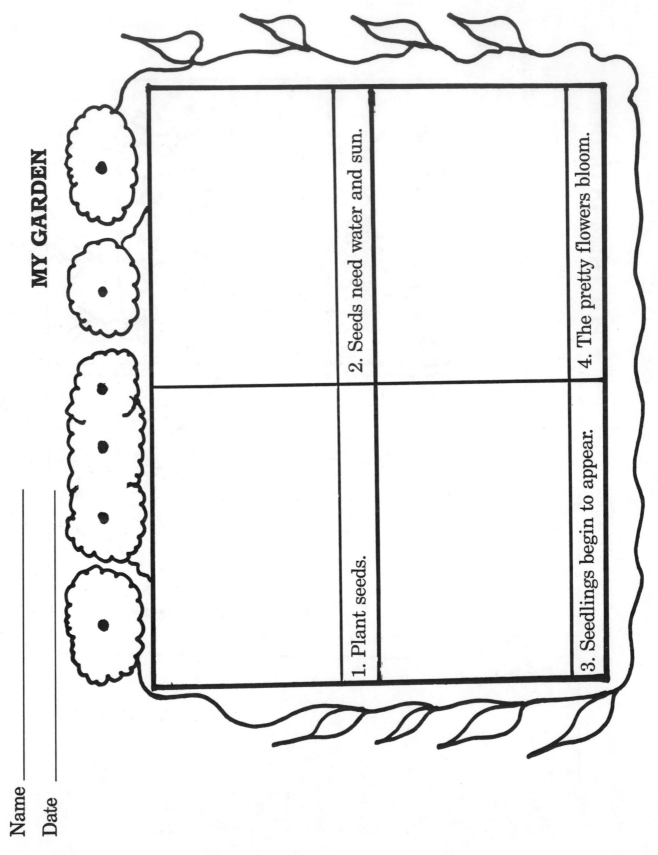

1. Plant seeds.

2. Seeds need water and sun.

3. Seedlings begin to appear.

4. The pretty flowers bloom.

Name _____

Date _____

A MEDICINE MAN MASK

What chants would a medicine man use? What advice would he give about plants that heal? Make this mask very colorful. Then cut it out and use string to make it fit around your face.

Name

Date

A SPACE-AGE MEDICINE PERSON MASK

Give a report on the future of medicine and people's health in the next century. Astronauts have brought tiny black dots back to Earth. How might these help improve people's health? Color and cut out mask. Wear when giving your report.

SAMP

Name _____

Date _____

COUNT THE FLOWER PETALS

Cut out the circled numerals at the bottom of this sheet. Count the petals on each flower and paste the correct circled numeral on the center part of each flower. When finished, color the flowers.

Name _____

Date _____

THE PARTS OF A SEED

Cut off the word strips at the bottom of the sheet.
Paste each label on the correct seed part.

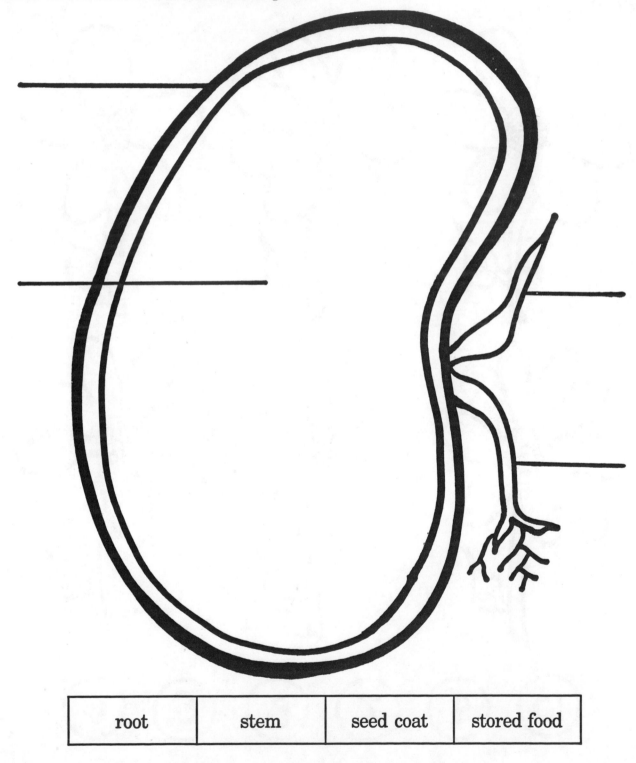

| root | stem | seed coat | stored food |

Name _____

Date _____

GARDEN EQUIPMENT

There are five pieces of equipment shown here that help you in your garden. Find each one and color it. Then put an X on the item not necessary for gardening.

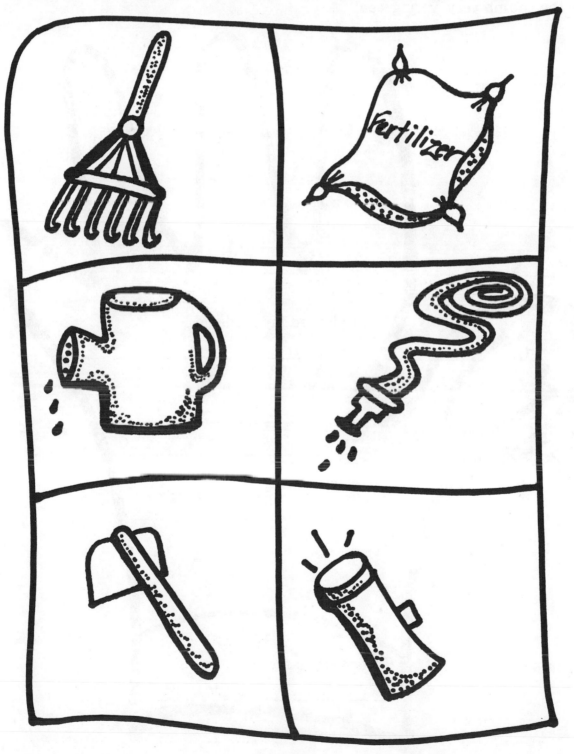

Name _____

Date _____

THE GREEN THUMB AWARD

When a person has very good luck with growing plants, we say that person has a "green thumb." Fill in the following information about your good luck with growing plants and color the thumb very, very green!

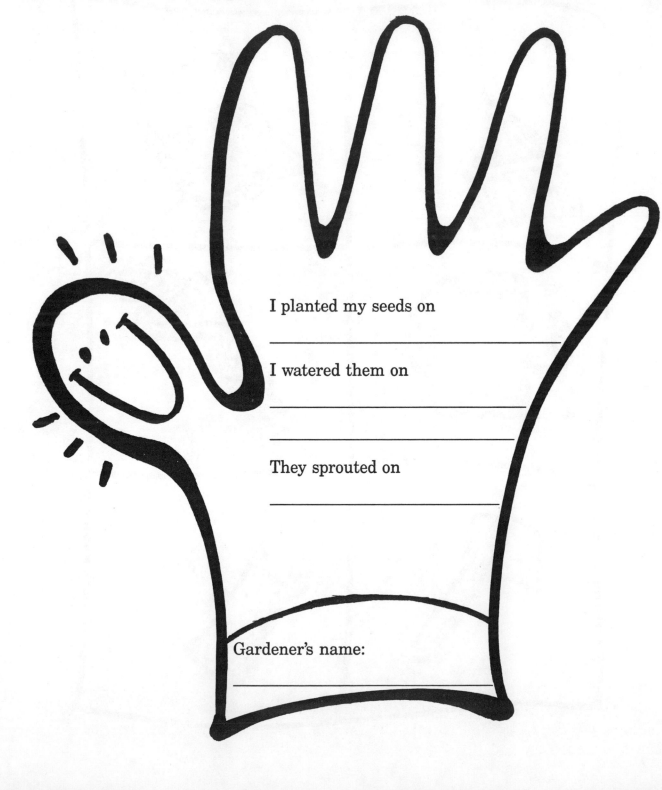

I planted my seeds on

_____

I watered them on

_____

_____

They sprouted on

_____

Gardener's name:

_____

Name _____

Date _____

PLAN AN HERB GARDEN

Select four herbs for your garden. Print one name in each rectangle, write its scientific name, and draw a diagram of the herb. On the back of this sheet, write the uses for each of the four herbs. Then find a recipe that uses each of the herbs and copy the recipes on other sheets of paper to share with friends.

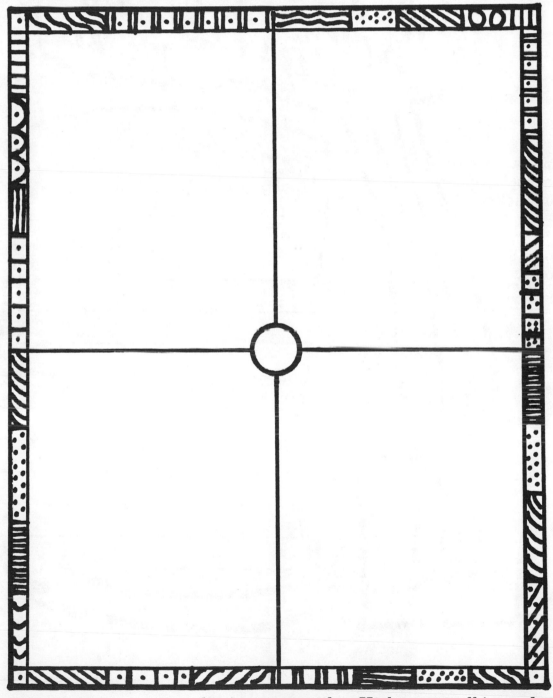

Perhaps you can carry out your plan in warm weather. Herbs grow well in good soil and can flourish in the ground, in pots, or in window boxes.

Name _____

Date _____

A GARDEN EXPERIMENT

We did an experiment with celery r colored water

Show what happened on the stalk.

Report:
_____
_____
_____
_____
_____
_____
_____
_____
_____
_____
_____

On the back, draw several pictures of the celery stalk. Draw the beginning, middle, and ending of the experiment. Be sure to label all work.

Name _____

Date _____

HELPFUL AND HARMFUL PLANTS

Plants That Heal

_____
_____
_____
_____
_____
_____
_____
_____
_____
_____
_____
_____
_____

Plants To Avoid

_____
_____
_____
_____
_____
_____
_____
_____
_____
_____
_____
_____
_____

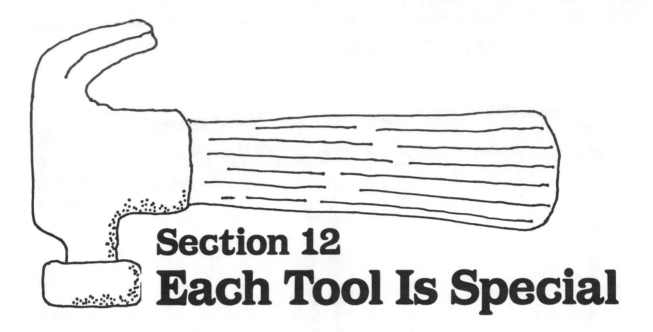

Section 12
Each Tool Is Special

Background Ideas and Other Helpful Things to Know

Tools are simple machines that people use to make their work easier. Tools are made by people and are used to perform tasks, with each job having its own special tools. We learn to use tools when we are just babies. Later we learn to use such tools as cups, spoons, and dishes. As we grow older, the kinds of tools we use and the tasks we perform with them change.

Tools change as time goes by. The refrigerators, record players, washing machines, telephones, and cars we use now are different from the ones people used 75 years ago. Some tools we use today will not be needed in the future, while new tools will have to be invented to do future jobs.

Activity Suggestions

Tools of the Trades. Each profession has its own special tools. Discuss and list with the children the tools of:

children	firefighters	bankers
parents	doctors	police officers
teachers	parachute jumpers	builders
carpenters	race car drivers	pilots

190

artists	painters	writers
plumbers	weavers	dancers
secretaries	lawyers	nurses
photographers	grocers	dentists
chefs	bookkeepers	engineers

Aside from the tools of children and parents, the rest of the tools that you list could be used by either men or women. We are fortunate today to be able to choose the kind of work we wish to do and be accepted in that profession.

Plant and Animal Tools. Do all living things use tools? Discuss the possibility of plants and animals using special tools not used by people. Children might share stories about animal tools (the elephant's trunk, the camel's hump, the beaver's tail, and the kangaroo's pouch). There is only one animal that actually makes its tools—the chimpanzee uses sticks and straws to catch ants to eat. It moistens the straw and inserts it down an ant hole. The chimp then lifts out the straw to eat the insects clinging to its tool.

Collage. Have the children make collages of pictures of tools cut from magazines. Display the collages around the classroom.

Tool Stations. Set up six stations in the classroom and let the students experience using different tools. The various stations could include:

saw and board and clamp

dustpan and small broom

screwdriver, board, screws, and clamp

hammer, board, and nails of different sizes

ruler, paper, and pencils (colored pencils, too)

stapler and small colored papers

Unusual Tools. Have a collection of unusual tools available and see if the children can guess what these tools help us do. Some examples are:

a staple remover	a potato masher
a grapefruit knife	a washboard
an apple corer	an electric pencil sharpener
a whisk	a fence post digger
a spatula	a cane
a tire jack	a drying rack

Homemade Tools. Let the children make simple tools from oaktag. A folded piece of oaktag can help lift; a flat piece can help scrape. Have a container of beans available to use with the folded tool and a pan of sand to use for the scraping tool.

Homemade Toy. Help each child make an old-fashioned toy using various tools. Help each child measure and cut a piece of dowel rod into a 6-inch length (ruler and saw). Sand both ends of the rod (sandpaper). Tie and glue a 9-inch piece of string to one end of the rod (string and glue). Tie a rubber jar ring to the other end of the string (jar ring). The object of the game is to catch the jar ring on the dowel rod by flipping the ring in the air.

Discuss why and how children used to make their own toys.

Machine Noises. Imitate the noises that machines and tools make. Create a human machine where each child is a special part of the machine that has a special motion and sound. Then ask each child to write a story about what he or she believes the machine will do to help us.

With the children, make a list of the words that describe the noises machines and tools might make.

Tool Pantomime. Guide the students in acting out the use of these tools:

saw	dishwasher
hammer	sink
silverware	stapler
jack	sponge
paintbrush	floor mop
pencil	mixer
broom	pancake flipper
vacuum cleaner	fishing pole
paper clip	scissors
chalk and eraser	stove
telephone	lawn mower
typewriter	iron

Tools at Home. Send home a letter to parents informing them that the class is beginning a study of tools. Tell them that the children will be identifying tools, determining how people use tools to make work easier, and learning that tools change because humans are constantly devising new ways of doing things. Let the parents know that there are activities they can do at home to reinforce discussions at school. Tell parents to

- Point out to their children the various tools found in the home and help the children learn the name and function of each.

- Play a game in which the parent and child name tools that belong in certain categories (tools for cooking, tools for building, tools for sewing).

- Give the child opportunities to demonstrate his or her ability to use tools.

- Share with the child any special tools the parent may use in his or her work away from home.

Categorizing Tools. Have each child bring a tool from home. Lay the tools in the middle of the circle of children and decide what categories the tools suggest. Lay the tools in rows, putting a small sign at the top of each row that names the category. Using 1-inch graph paper, have the children graph the tools in each row by writing the word at the top of the row and coloring in the correct number of squares.

Activity Sheets for
EACH TOOL IS SPECIAL

Name _____

Date _____

CLASSIFY THE TOOLS

Certain tools help you do special jobs. Color each tool below. Then cut each box apart and separate the tools into three categories—those that would be used at home, those that would be used at school, and those that could be used in both places.

Name _____

Date _____

I KNOW THESE TOOLS

In each box below, draw a tool you have at home or a tool that your mom or dad uses at work.

Name _____

Date _____

THE JOBS OF TOOLS

Tools can help you cut, lift, and push. Color the tools at the bottom of the page. Then cut them out and paste each one in the correct column. How many tools are there in each column? Can you think of others that would fit in each column? One of the tools below does all three jobs! Can you tell which one?

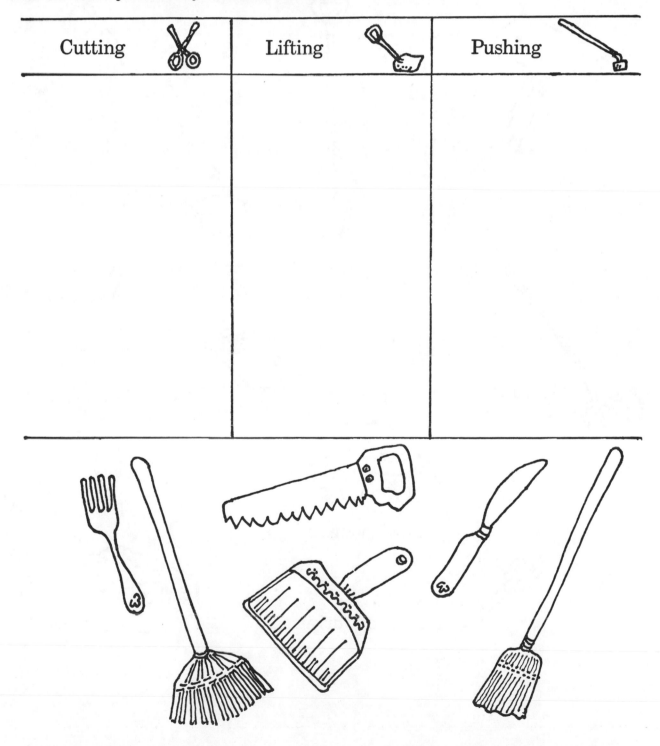

Cutting		Lifting		Pushing	

Name _____

Date _____

FILL IN THE MISSING LETTERS

Look at each tool below and fill in the missing letters in its name. When you've finished, color the tools.

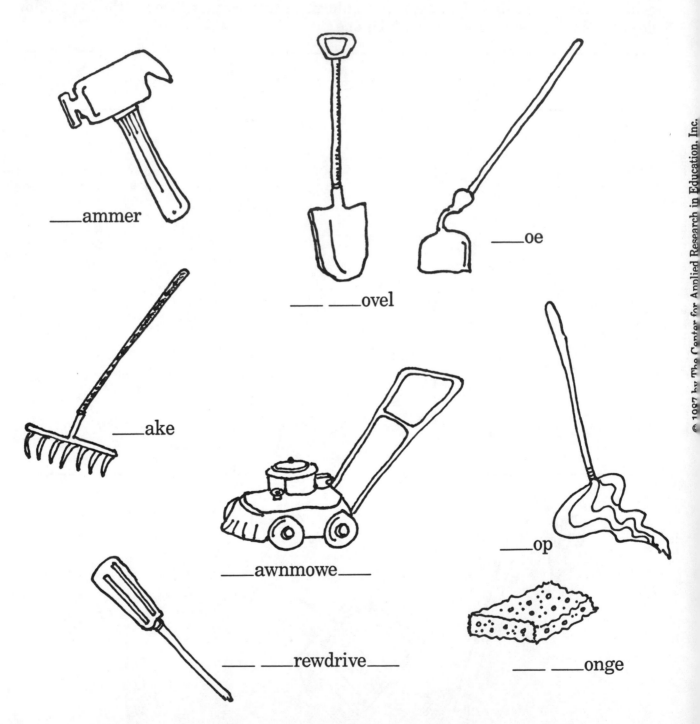

___ammer

___ ___ovel

___oe

___ake

___awnmowe___

___op

___ ___rewdrive___

___ ___onge

Name _____

Date _____

A PAINTBRUSH PARAGRAPH

How would you feel if you were a paintbrush? What would you like to paint and what colors would you use? Write your thoughts on this paintbrush and think of a good title for your story. Use the back of this sheet if you need more space to write.

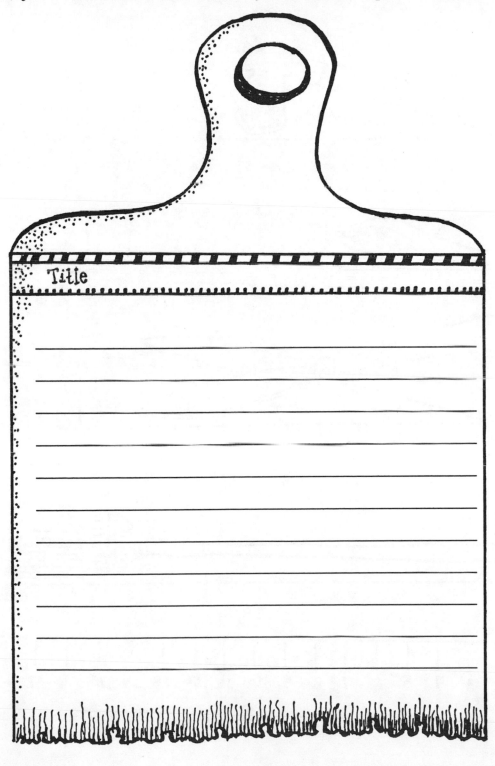

Title

Name _____

Date _____

MEASURE THE TOOLS IN METRIC

A ruler is a tool. Cut out the ruler at the bottom of this sheet and use it to measure the other tools on this page. Write the correct number of centimeters in the box next to each tool. Which tool is the longest? Which tool is the shortest?

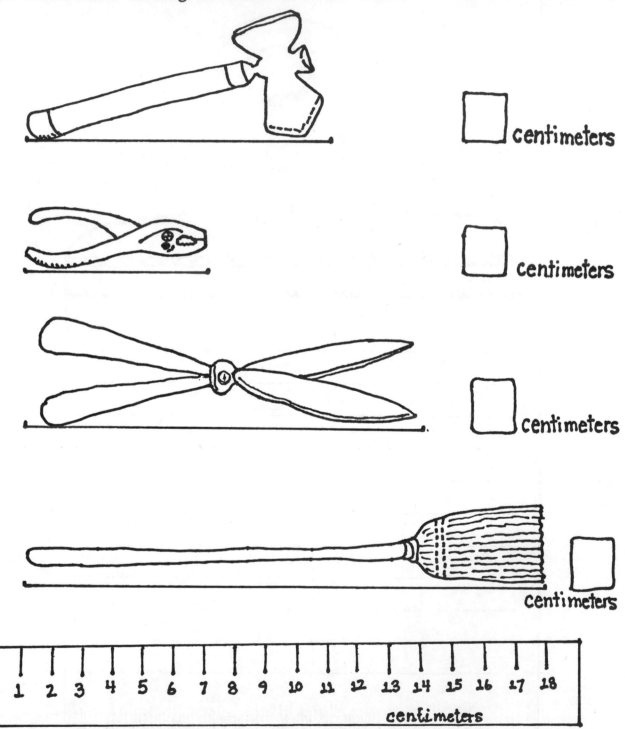

☐ centimeters

☐ centimeters

☐ centimeters

☐ centimeters

Name _____

Date _____

ADD THE NAILS

Cut apart the number sentences at the bottom of the page and paste the correct one under each hammer. Then complete the equations. When you're finished, color the smallest number of nails blue and color the biggest number of nails red.

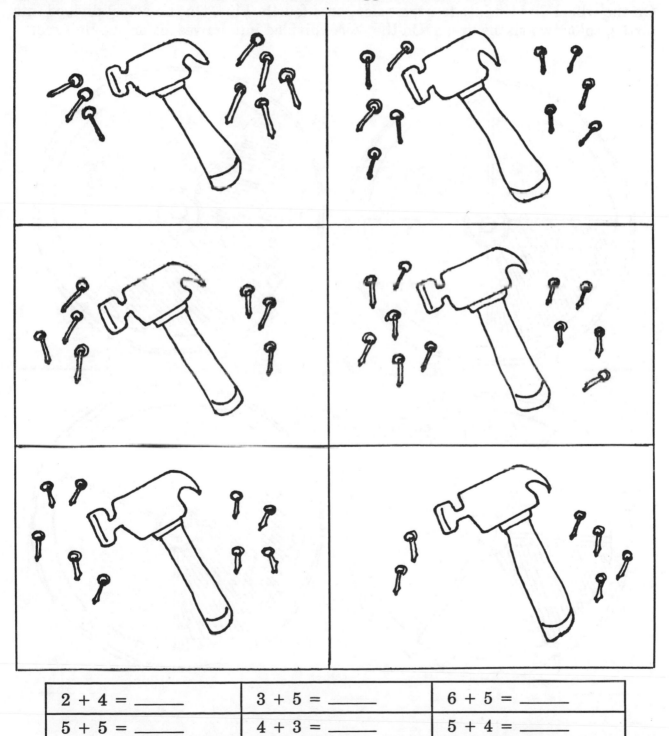

| 2 + 4 = _____ | 3 + 5 = _____ | 6 + 5 = _____ |
| 5 + 5 = _____ | 4 + 3 = _____ | 5 + 4 = _____ |

Name _____

Date _____

WHEEL FRACTIONS

Wheels are tools that help machines move. The wheels below are divided into equal parts. On the line next to each wheel, write the fraction for the shaded part of the whole wheel. Then do the following: on the wheel divided into thirds, color one-third yellow. On the wheel divided into fourths, color three-fourths blue. On the wheel divided into sixths, color two-sixths green. On the wheel divided into halves, color one-half red.

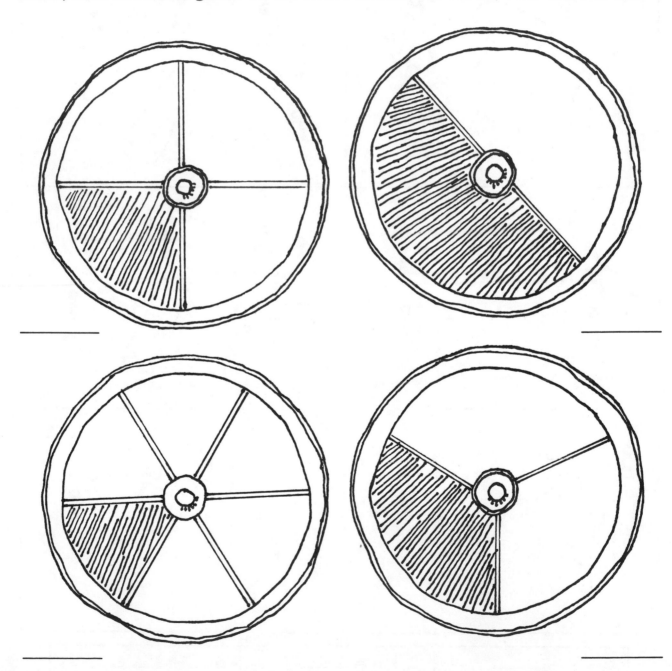

Name _____

Date _____

DRAW AN INCLINED PLANE

An inclined plane is a machine that is used as a tool to make going up and coming down much easier. A slanting board can be an inclined plane. Stairsteps can also be an inclined plane.

In each box below, there is a toy truck at the top of each inclined plane. If the board is higher, the slope is greater and the truck will roll faster. Follow the directions in the boxes on the right.

Draw an inclined plane and a truck that will roll faster than the one on the left.

Draw an inclined plane and a truck that will roll slower than the one on the left.

Draw an inclined plane and a truck that will roll slower than the one on the left.

Name _____

Date _____

WHICH TOOLS?

Levers, inclined planes, and wheels all help to make work easier. Follow the directions in each box below. When you're finished, color the tools.

Circle the tools that are levers.

Circle the tools that are inclined planes.

Circle the tools that use wheels to make them work.

Name _____

Date _____

LABEL THE LEVERS

A lever is a tool that helps to lift things. There are two numbers in each box below. Look inside the base of each lever at the greater than (>) or less than (<) sign. Write the correct number in each box on the levers. The first one has been done for you. When you've finished, decide whether the larger number is higher or lower on the lever.

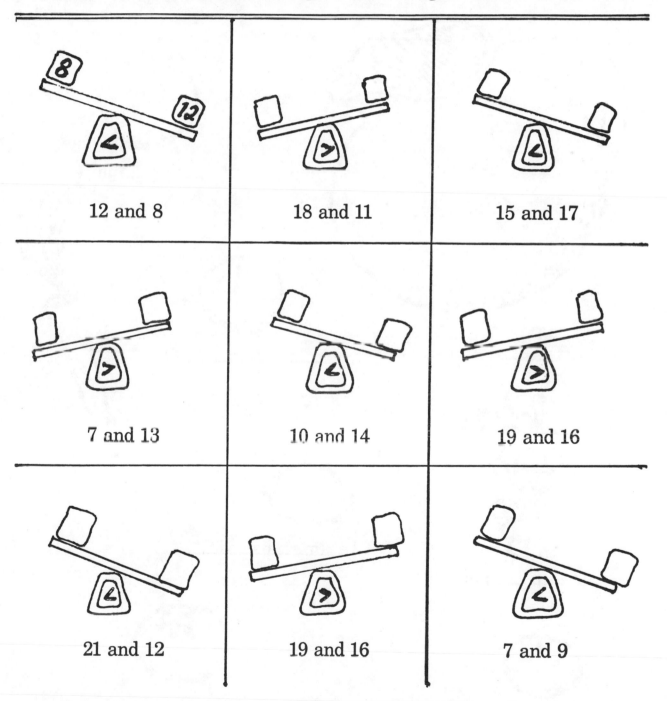

12 and 8

18 and 11

15 and 17

7 and 13

10 and 14

19 and 16

21 and 12

19 and 16

7 and 9

Name _____

Date _____

FILL IN THE MISSING VOWELS

A pitcher is a tool used to pour liquids. You might fill this pitcher with juice made from any of the fruits and vegetables on this page. Fill in the missing vowels in each word and then color the pictures.

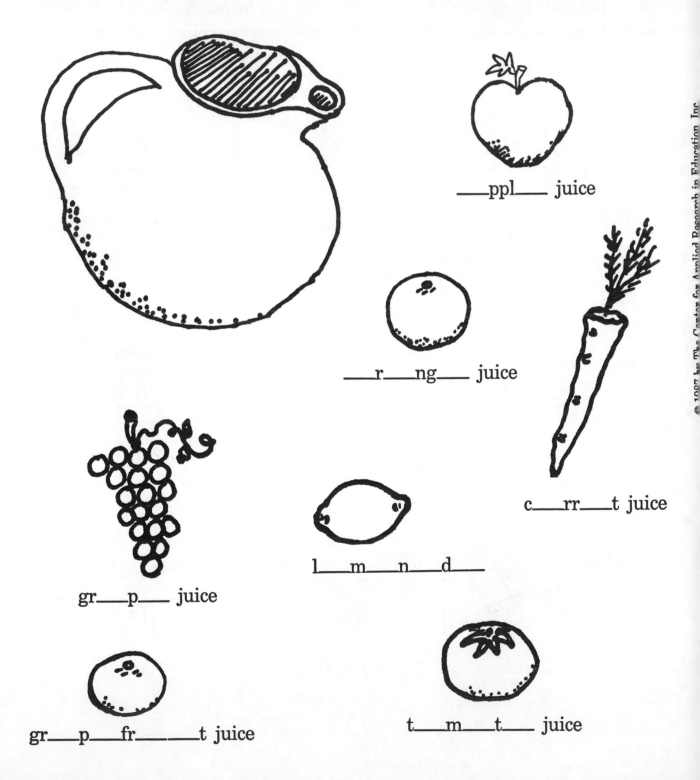

___ppl___ juice

___r___ng___ juice

c___rr___t juice

gr___p___ juice

l___m___n___d___

gr___p___fr___t juice

t___m___t___ juice

Section 13
TRANSPORTATION MAKES THE WORLD GO 'ROUND

Background Ideas and Other Helpful Things to Know

People first transported items by pulling or lugging them themselves. Later, animals were used to help carry and pull heavy loads. The loads were either strapped onto the animals' backs or attached to a harness and pulled. The actual date of the invention of the wheel is not known, but it revolutionized transportation. Now things could be piled onto carts or wagons and transported in quantities by horses, mules, and other domestic animals either singly or in teams.

With the invention of the engine, the "horseless carriage" came upon the scene. By 1927, about 15 million Model T automobiles had been sold. Cars have become much more streamlined and complicated since then.

Some other forms of transportation by wheel include bicycles, unicycles, motorcycles, trucks, buses, tractors, trains, steamboats, airplanes, jets, helicopters, scooters, and roller skates. Section 13 deals with transportation on land that has been made possible by the discovery of the wheel.

Activity Suggestions

Wheels Bulletin Board. From bright red construction paper or glossy red paper, cut out wheels of various shapes and sizes and place them randomly on a large bulletin board with a white background. Then have the children work together to create a variety of vehicles from the wheels. (A red/white/black color scheme is striking and places the accent on the wheels. The children can work with a black felt tip or black crayon.) Since children "see" various things in the wheels, this is an activity that can also be done individually. (See Activity Sheet 13–10.)

Trucks. Some trucks are extremely specialized, such as fire trucks, garbage trucks, telephone trucks, refrigeration trucks, and tow trucks. Discuss what it is that makes these trucks "special." Ask the children to cut out magazine pictures of trucks and make a photo montage on a large sheet of heavy paper. How many 18-wheelers can the children find?

Hook and Ladder, Hose, and Crow's-Nest. Arrange to visit the fire station and have a firefighter explain the functions of the fire truck to the class, or arrange to have the firefighter bring the truck to the playground at your school for about an hour. This is a good activity during Fire Prevention Week. Ask the firefighter to demonstrate the hook and ladder. Also, ask the firefighter to explain some fire prevention rules (Stop, Drop, Roll). Later, have the children discuss and plan fire escape routes at home with parents or babysitters. (See Activity Sheet 13–1.)

Invent a Bike. The first two-wheel bicycle with pedals was built in the 1800s. Today we have streamlined bicycles with brakes on the handlebars and a variety of speeds, such as 3-speed or 10-speed. What will the bicycle of the year 2000 be like? Have the students become inventors and plan the future bicycle on paper. Ask them to include safety devices as well as futuristic conveniences. Remember, the age and development level of your students will help to determine the application of science and technology. (See Activity Sheet 13–2.)

The Recreational Vehicle Plan. Have the children select a city and state as their point of departure and a city and state as their destination. Then get out all of your maps for this plan. (Auto clubs and travel agencies are invaluable sources for this activity.) Guide the children in listing all of the route numbers they will take. How many large cities will they bypass? (List them.) Is the entire class taking the same route or will different groups take different routes? (Decide this.) How many miles will they travel? (Compute this.) How many states will they travel through? (List them.) How many miles will they travel within each state? (Compute this.) Have the children draw and label their routes on a 12-by-18-inch sheet of manila paper.

As an additional math activity, ask, "How many miles to the gallon does the van get?" "How many stops for gasoline will you need to make along the way?" "How many stops will you take along the way for food, rest, overnight sleeping?" "Will you visit any historic sights along the routes?" "Will you take any detours to visit special places nearby?" This activity will require a lot of group problem solving.

Brainstorming. Divide the class into smaller groups of three to five students. Select one person in each group as the "recorder" and give that person paper and pencil. Time the groups for five minutes as they list as many transportation vehicles as they can think of. Remind students to speak quietly because they don't want to "give away" information to another group. (You'll find the children usually end up whispering during this activity.) After five minutes, have each recorder report the vehicles listed. Make a master list from this and print it on a huge chart in the room. OPTIONAL: Have the students draw the vehicles on the chart next to the name.

Open/Closed. Have the students make a list of all "open" vehicles (bicycle, motorcycle, and so on) and then a list of all the "closed" vehicles (auto, bus, and so on). Some vehicles may fit into either category, so if the students can justify their answer, accept it.

Speeding Along. Explain the concept of miles per hour (mph). For example, 55 mph means that if you travel at a steady speed of 55 for one hour, you will have traveled a distance of 55 miles in one hour. The following vehicles travel at these speeds:

Horse-drawn chariot	20 mph
Steam railroad engine	60 mph
Gasoline-powered automobile	55 mph
Japanese Tokaido Express Train, "The Bullet"	160 mph

This information enables you and your students to do many math problems together using the chalkboard. For example, "How long would it take to travel 120 miles by chariot? by railroad? by 'The Bullet'?"

At the beginning of each day, select a different vehicle for travel. At the end of each day (agree on the length of time), see how far the children have "traveled." (Students can work on this when they "can't find anything to do"!)

			Total Hours in School	Total Distance
Monday	car	55 mph	_____	_____
Tuesday	Chariot	20 mph	_____	_____
Wednesday	The Bullet	160 mph	_____	_____
Thursday	18-wheeler	60 mph	_____	_____
Friday	race car	200 mph	_____	_____

This can be the beginning of a "Math Puzzle-of-the-Day" for students, which brings the aspect of problem solving in mathematics into the curriculum as a stimulating approach to learning.

Sports Speed. Some of the children, especially older students, may be interested in learning more about the Indianapolis 500 (auto racing) or the Kentucky Derby (horse racing). These are two annual events where speed is the key. Sports events from other countries may be explored, such as the MTT (Isle of Man) Tourist Trophy in Great Britain (motorcycle racing). Use the library as a resource.

This may also lead the learner to find out about timing in sports with and without wheels; for example, cycling (45 mph), downhill skiing (60 to 100 mph), and sky diving (185 mph, steady fall).

Speed in sports also requires physical fitness, endurance, discipline, practice, and other skills. Ask: "What local events (such as a marathon walk, marathon run, bike ride, boat race) do you have in your area where speed is a prime factor?" Check for more information with the sports editor of the local newspaper, who might be able to recommend local resources that you can contact. Invite a coach or high school sports participant to your classroom for an information session.

Remember, both girls and boys enjoy the learning of mathematics via sports. Experienced teachers have capitalized upon the Olympics as a rich source of mathematical learning and application.

Our Shrinking World. The distance around the earth is extremely long. At one time the mail was delivered in this country by Pony Express, then by stagecoach, then train, bus, truck, ship, and eventually by airplane. Today, news bulletins are beamed via satellite. (When President Lincoln was shot in 1864, it took two weeks for the news to reach Europe. When President Reagan was shot in 1981, an editor in Europe heard the news on television via satellite and telephoned an editor in New York City for verification. The New York City editor, busy at work in his office, hadn't heard the news. So, he heard from Europe that the president of his own country was shot!)

Ask the children what the speeding up of transportation (two days for a plane to fly around the world) and communication (instantaneous) has done to our world in terms of the following:

travel	language	measurement	food
money	entertainment	health	education
research	inventions	germs	space

You might have the students report in terms of perspective (past, present, future) or contrast (past and present) or some other form. Reports may be written and distributed via newspaper (ditto), broadcast via tape recorder, or given orally as a live television news report.

Signs and Signals. Traffic signals play an important part in transportation. Ask: "What are their uses?" "What are the shapes and colors?" "What do the symbols mean?" When the children have compiled their list, write a class rebus story using as many of the signs as you can. Older students may want to investigate the international signs and create some of their own.

Tracks and Treads. Tire treads are designed to get the most traction, such as diagonal lines for use on soft ground. While it is not feasible to get actual samples of tire treads from tractors, tractor-trailers, buses, and cars, your students might be able to get a good look at the tread on a bicycle wheel. Flatten out a piece of plasticene with the palm of your hand, place it on the tire, press gently, and remove it carefully. This will show the tread imprint.

Since walking is a means of transportation, take a tread imprint of children's athletic shoes. Have a student remove his or her sneaker and place it in a shallow amount of water (just enough to wet the sole). Remove the sneaker from the water, shake it gently, and blot it on a piece of colored 9-by-12-inch construction paper. Remove the sneaker from the paper and trace around the tread with a dark crayon before the design dries. These treads can be displayed on a bulletin board. How many ways can the students classify them? Look for similarities and patterns.

Windshield Wipers. The windshield of a vehicle is just that—a shield from the wind and flying dust, dirt, and debris. Windshield wipers and spray become important in keeping the field of vision clear. Have the students show with hand and arm motion just how the windshield wipers operate on a car. Pretend their arms are the windshield wipers and show the different patterns. Using the arm motions, also show "fast," "slow," and "delayed." Remind the children to notice the windshield wipers on the school bus, family car, neighbor's car, and so on.

A Giant Compass. You need a magnet, needle, cork, bowl of water, markers, compasses, construction paper, and scissors. *Directions:* Rub the magnet along the needle, starting at the eye end and going toward the point. Repeat this 30 times. The needle should now be magnetic. Spear the needle through the cork until it balances in water. When it comes to rest, the needle is pointing north (N). Bring in several types of compasses (for hiking, backpacking, bicycling, car compass, and so on) to check.

Now the students are ready for some preliminary map skills. What is to the north of the school? to the south? to the east? to the west? Guide the children in making maps of the school neighborhood showing the four directions. Then make a giant map of the classroom on paper. Cut out giant letters of N, S, E, and W and place them accurately around the room. Turn your room into a compass by referring to events that are taking place in the north end, a special interest area in the west end, and so on. NOTE: With older children, you can talk about Northeast, Northwest, Southeast, and Southwest.

Activity Sheets for
TRANSPORTATION
MAKES THE WORLD
GO 'ROUND

Name _____

Date _____

FIRE ESCAPE ROUTES

First, draw your classroom fire escapes. SHH! No talking! Then draw the fire escape route for your home. Can you identify all the firefighting equipment at the bottom of this page? Color each piece.

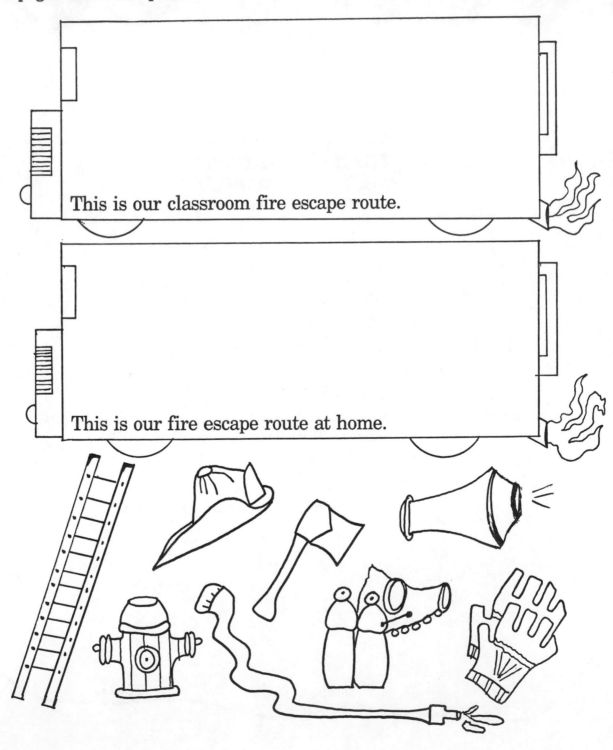

This is our classroom fire escape route.

This is our fire escape route at home.

Name _____

Date _____

INVENT A BICYCLE

Carefully observe a bicycle and note the moving parts as well as the parts that remain still. What will the bicycle look like 100 years from now? Draw your plan of the future bicycle here and give it a name. Then, on the lines below, explain how the bicycle will work. Use the back of this sheet if you need more space to write.

The bicycle of the future will be called _____.

Name _____

Date _____

THE TRAFFIC LIGHT

This light sends signals by color to drivers and pedestrians. Color the lights RED, YELLOW, and GREEN. Then cut out the circles at the bottom of this page that tell what each color means. Paste the circles on the lines next to the lights.

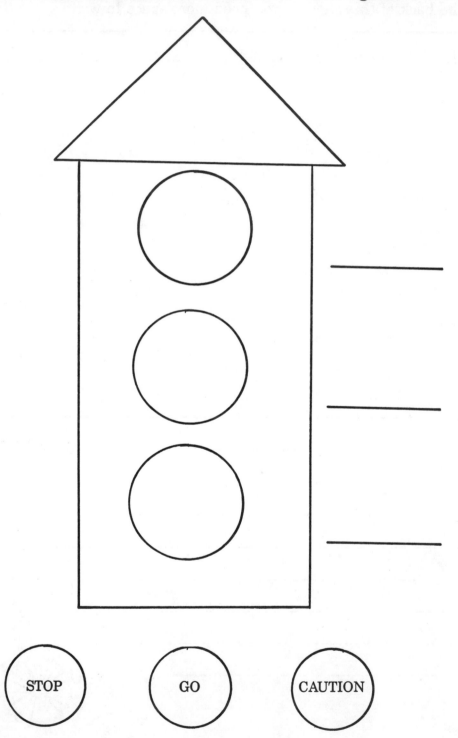

STOP   GO   CAUTION

Name _____

Date _____

TRAVELOGUE

Congratulations! You have just won this van and a trip for a week. Your only cost will be for fuel. First, select your destination. Then chart your daily mileage from city to city and keep track of your fuel costs. Have a good trip!

From: _____   To: _____   Total Miles: _____

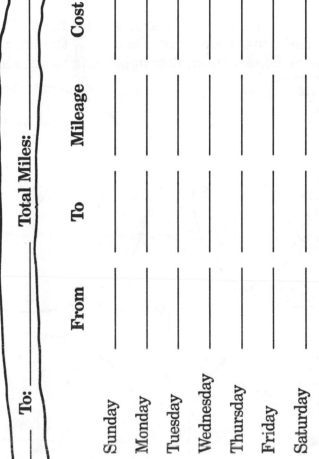

	From	To	Mileage	Cost
Sunday	_____	_____	_____	_____
Monday	_____	_____	_____	_____
Tuesday	_____	_____	_____	_____
Wednesday	_____	_____	_____	_____
Thursday	_____	_____	_____	_____
Friday	_____	_____	_____	_____
Saturday	_____	_____	_____	_____
			Total:	_____

On the back of this sheet, show and label three interesting sights you see along the way.

Name _____

Date _____

COMPLETE THE CLOCKS

Some clocks are round and the hands go around the face of the clock. Write the remaining numerals on the face of each clock. Then draw the hands to show the correct time. The first one has been done for you. Remember, one hand is longer than the other.

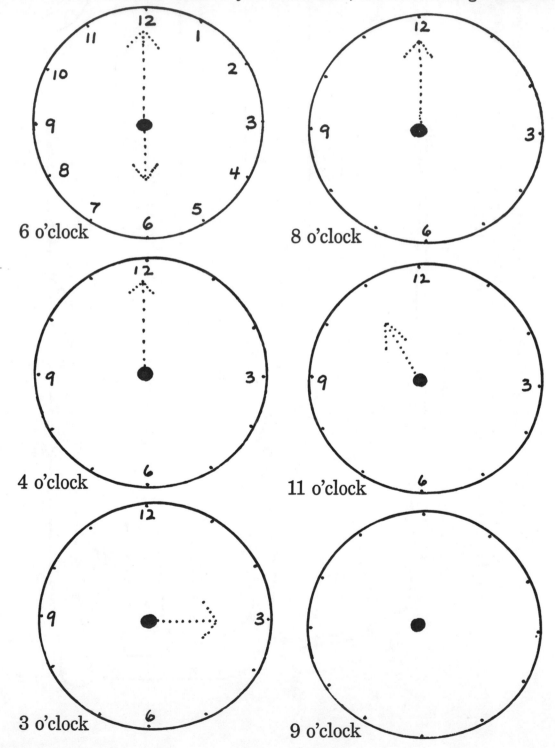

6 o'clock   8 o'clock

4 o'clock   11 o'clock

3 o'clock   9 o'clock

Name _____

Date _____

ADDITION MATH WHEELS

Complete the following math wheels for addition. Two in the first one have been done for you.

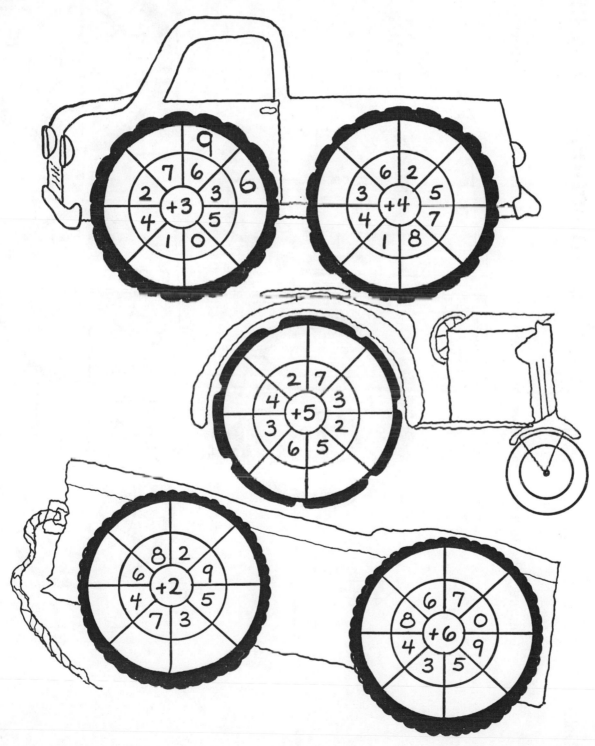

SUBTRACTION MATH WHEELS

Name

Date

Complete the following math wheels for subtraction. One in the first wheel has been done for you.

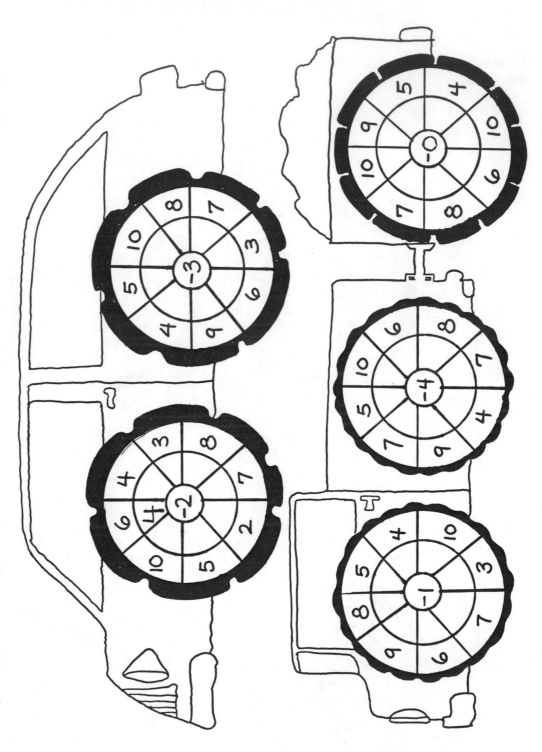

Name _____

Date _____

MAKE YOUR OWN MATH WHEELS

Here's your chance to make your own math wheels—and vehicles, too! Share these wheels with your classmates.

Name _____

Date _____

TRAFFIC SYMBOLS

Traffic signs convey very important information. Be on the lookout for traffic signs in your neighborhood!

MATCH THE SHAPE	MATCH THE TRAFFIC SYMBOL

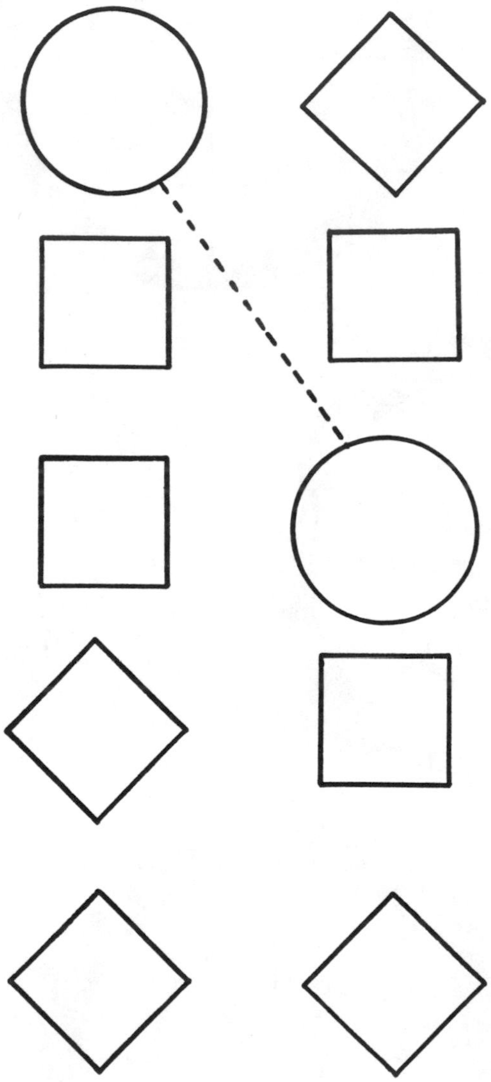

What are these shapes called?

What do these symbols mean?
What are the shapes of the signs?

AND THE WHEELS GO 'ROUND AND 'ROUND

See how many different vehicles you can draw to fit the sets of wheels below. Look at some pictures of trucks, trains, buses, cars, tractors, and other specific vehicles to help you get started. Guide your pencil as carefully as you would drive and share your finished vehicles with your classmates. (Don't forget to make the wheels interesting!)

Name

Date

Section 14

TREES: THE GIANTS OF NATURE

Background Ideas and Other Helpful Things to Know

There are two general types of trees: evergreen (conifer) and broadleaf (deciduous). Most evergreens have needles and some have cones. Because evergreens lose their needles a few at a time instead of all at once, they always look green. Broadleafs, on the other hand, change color in autumn and put on an artistic display in the sky. During this burst of color, the leaves fall to the ground. In the winter when the trees look bare, we say they are dormant. In the spring, buds appear and new green leaves are formed. The tree keeps its green foliage during the summer until the cycle repeats in autumn.

Trees are the oldest living things in the world. A tree is a plant with roots, stem, seeds, and leaves. The leaves get their energy from sunlight to make food for all parts of the tree (a process called photosynthesis). Some trees can grow to be 300 feet tall!

During this section, children will gain a greater appreciation of the usefulness of trees, how much we depend upon them, and a heightened awareness and sensitivity to trees (texture of bark, shapes of leaves, and types of seeds) in their immediate environment.

Activity Suggestions

Measuring a Giant. The oldest and biggest living things on earth are the giant redwood and sequoia trees in California, which can grow to 365 feet in height! To determine how tall that is, equate it with one foot (12 inches) for every day of the year. Get a huge ball of string and measure one foot of it; then repeat this 365 times. (Tie strings together as the measured ball grows, and label periodically such as 20 feet, 50 feet, 100 feet.) Then take this giant ball of string onto the playground and carefully unwind it so that the students can get some idea of the enormous size. Have students walk along it or sit along it at 5-foot or 10-foot intervals. Ask: "How tall is it in comparison to the flagpole outside the school building?" "How many synonyms can you find and list for BIG?" (Huge, enormous, and gigantic are some examples.) If you do the measuring in the month that contains 30 days, you can say that a "Sequoia is 12 times the month of September" or "12 times the month of April." In what other ways can the children describe it with colorful language?

Two Types of Trees. All students can learn that there are two types of trees and, depending upon their age and grade level, they can learn that the two categories are evergreen (conifer) and broadleaf (deciduous).

Set up a Science Table or Science Corner in the room and collect samples of needles and leaves.

Evergreen

White pine—five needles in a bundle. Ask the children to make a list of things that come in five's (five people in a family, five buttons on the television set, five fingers, five toes, and so on).

Red pine—two needles together. Have the children make a list of things that come in two's (or pairs).

Spruce—four sides on each needle. Teach the concept of four sides. What examples can be found in the room of four-sided items? Ask the children to be on the alert for four-sided items in nature and, if possible, bring them in for the Science Table.

Broadleafs

Maple, oak, ash, cottonwood, holly, elm, and so on. Make a shapeboard containing the leaves. Have students bring in sample leaves and keep them in a basket. Have the children categorize them by holding the actual leaf up to the shape of the leaf.

Points. Juniper trees have very sharp, pointed needles. If you cannot get a sample, sharpen a pencil and have the students gently feel the point. Discuss the things in our environment that are pointed (compass, hands on a clock, knitting needles, pins, cactus, rose thorns, teasels, and so on).

Guide the children in making the following:

- an illustrated book of "Useful Points" (needles, pencils, pens, scissors, and so on)
- a list of all the arrows we see on signs (What are they pointing to?)
- a list of the way in which we use the word "point" in our language (How many can you remember or discover?)

Get to the point	Point of view
Point the way	The point is
Let me point out	What's the point?
Do you get the point?	The main point is
That's beside the point	In point of fact

Sugar Maple Sampling. Let the children taste a sample of maple syrup or maple candy. If you live in a part of the country where sugar maples are plentiful, go with the children to see the trees during the gathering of the sap. A dab of maple sugar on snow, otherwise known as snow cones, has always been considered a delicacy!

Tree Collage. Help the students collect natural items from trees (leaves, nuts, seeds, needles, pine cones) and glue them to a large piece of cardboard in an all-over scatter pattern. When the glue has dried, spray paint in splotches using green, red, and orange. Guide the children in creating a border from oaktag and gluing or stapling it around the edges of the cardboard. Prop the large collage in a corner, bring in large pillows, set up a rustic basket filled with good books about trees, and encourage the students to read in this area.

Go on a Tree-Bark Walk. Bark is the outer covering of the woody stems, branches, and trunks of trees, as opposed to the cambium and inner wood. Bark comes in a wide variety of textures (compare the sugar maple and the shagbark hickory) and a wide variety of colors (compare the white birch with various tones of brown, gray, and black bark). Go on a tree walk with the children to examine the bark patterns and to do bark rubbings. Place a 9-by-12-inch piece of paper firmly against a tree. Use the broad length of a crayon to rub back and forth on the paper repeatedly until the bark design shows on the paper. Begin a bark collection from fallen tree branches. Caution the children to respect trees and to "not be a moose" (a moose strips the bark and eats it, causing damage to the tree).

Thanks to the Generous Trees. Make a gigantic construction paper tree for the bulletin board. Each day discuss a different part of the tree with the students and explore the products that are derived from that particular part of the tree. For example:

Wood

lumber (furniture, wooden toys, utensils, rulers, clothespins, pencils, bowls, and so on)

Pulp

paper (napkins, bags, cups, books, magazines, envelopes, and so on)

Seeds

nuts, coconut, coffee, cocoa, and so on

Cellulose

derived from the wood and used in making plastic products and rayon cloth

Each day, have the children bring in sample items for the tree, label them, and hang them on the tree with staples, thumbtacks, or string and thumbtacks.

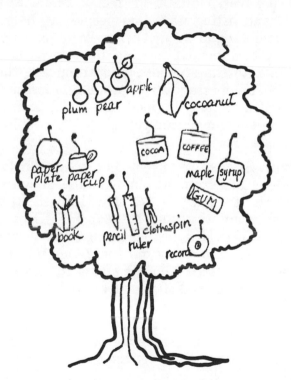

This bulletin board is effective because it creates a great deal of interest as the tree begins to bulge with objects that the children are encouraged to keep bringing in. The visual effect helps to create an appreciation of the value of trees and of their usefulness in our lives. And, the bigger the tree, the more items it can hold—and the greater the impact upon the classroom learning environment.

Splatter Painting. You need a flat leaf (real or oaktag), tempera paint, toothbrush, 3-by-3-inch screen, 9-by-12-inch construction paper, and smocks. *Directions:* Place the leaf on a sheet of construction paper. Dip the toothbrush in tempera paint (not too much). Hold the screen right over the leaf with one hand. With the other hand, brush slowly back and forth on the screen so that the paint splatters under it and lands on and around the leaf. (Or have the children work in pairs or with partners so that one child holds the screen while the other child brushes.) A silhouette of the leaf appears when the leaf is removed.

Prevent Forest Fires. No unit on trees is complete without mentioning "Smokey the Bear" and listing ways that people can help prevent forest fires when camping or picnicking in wooded areas. Write to one of the national parks for fire prevention information. If possible, invite a park ranger or state park representative to talk to the students, and encourage the children to make posters that send a visual message about preventing forest fires. Smokey can be made from a piece of fake fur (obtained from a fabric shop), and the leaping flames can be made more menacing by gluing or stapling crackling orange cellophane to the poster.

Measuring with Sticks. You need eight or nine fairly straight tree sticks about one foot in length. *Directions:* Individually or with partners, have the children "measure" with the sticks. Ask: "How many sticks high is the counter?" "The desk top?" "How many sticks long is the room?" "Does the answer vary with the different sticks?" It should! This measuring is an approximation.

How do we measure with a crooked stick? One solution is to get a ball of string. Place the end of the string on one end of the stick and tape it securely. Guide the string to the other end of the stick until it is taut, cut it, and tape it securely. Next, measure the string with a straight ruler. By measuring the straight string with a ruler, you get a closer approximation of the length of the stick. This points to (and reinforces) the necessity for standard measurement for accurate work in mathematics. Now let the children measure with the strings and see if the answers are the same.

Acid Rain. As fossil fuels are burning, large amounts of waste products are given off. These wastes are sulfur dioxide (SO_2) and nitrogen oxides (NO_x). In the atmosphere, these gases can combine with oxygen and water to form sulfuric acid and nitric acid, which we know as "acid rain" when it falls to earth. One result of acid rain could be deforestation, or the eventual destruction of our precious natural resource—forests. What is being done about this problem? Write a class letter to your congressional representative, state senator, or to the Environmental Protection Agency, Washington, D.C., to get some possible answers.

Arbor Day. This is the day set aside in the spring to honor trees. It is a time when your students can plant a real tree in the soil. Look at the calendar and find out when Arbor Day falls this year. Does your school plan to plant a tree? (Some PTAs fund this project). Did you know that the practice of planting trees on this day is said to have originated in the state of Nebraska? Look up "arbor" in the dictionary to find out its meaning.

A Tree and Leaf Identification Book. Collect a wide variety of leaf shapes. (Autumn is an especially good time to do this.) Place each leaf between two pieces of wax paper, cover with a cloth, and press with a warm iron. (CAUTION: Do this activity only under adult supervision and with one child at a time.) Help the children to categorize leaves, staple them in a scrap book, and label each one. This book can be made from colorful sheets of construction paper stapled together along the edge or top. Book cover and pages could be in the shape of a giant leaf.

A Tree-Tasting Party. Have a tasting party of fruits that grow on trees. Cut and quarter several varieties of fruit, such as apples, pears, plums, peaches, and cherries. Include one or two unusual fruits, such as kiwi, lichi, pomegranate, or kumquats. In honor of the tree, be sure to serve the fruit on paper plates, use plastic forks, and serve your beverage (apple juice, orange juice, grapefruit juice) in a paper cup. Don't forget the paper napkins. Can the children identify the fruits by smell alone?

Activity Sheets for
THE GIANTS OF NATURE

Name _____

Date _____

THE FOUR SEASONS

The maple tree is one of the prettiest of all trees. Show how it looks during the four seasons.

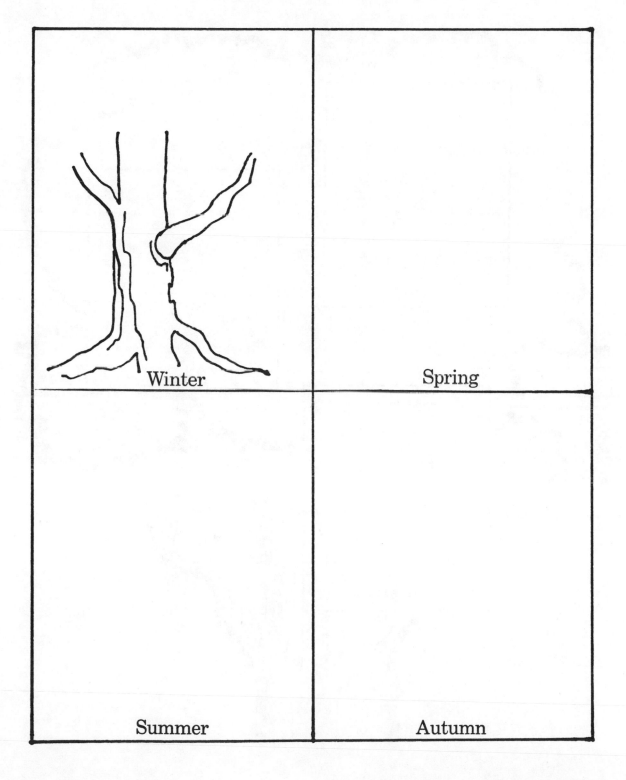

Name _____

Date _____

THANKS TO TREES

Many items we use every day come from trees.
Draw and label five byproducts in each box.

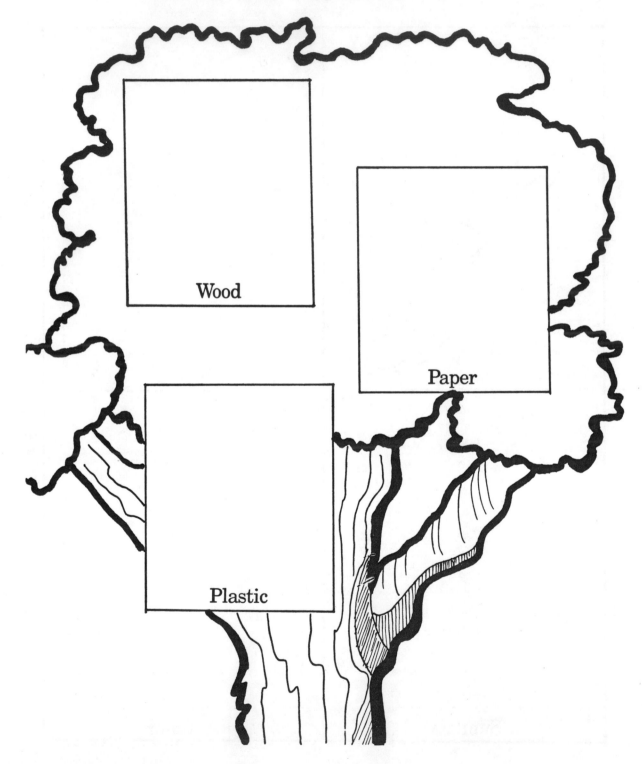

Wood

Paper

Plastic

Name _____

Date _____

WHAT'S THE LEAF?

Find the matching leaf shape at the bottom of this page. Cut out the strip and paste it under the leaf that looks the same.

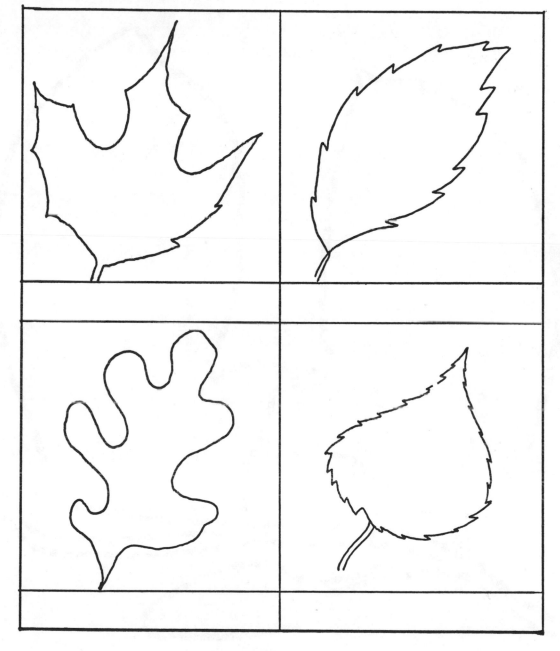

Name _____

Date _____

THE SASSAFRAS TREE

Leaves of the sassafras tree can look like this 〇 or this 🌿 or they can be shaped like mittens 🌿🌿 . Decorate the "mitten tree" here.

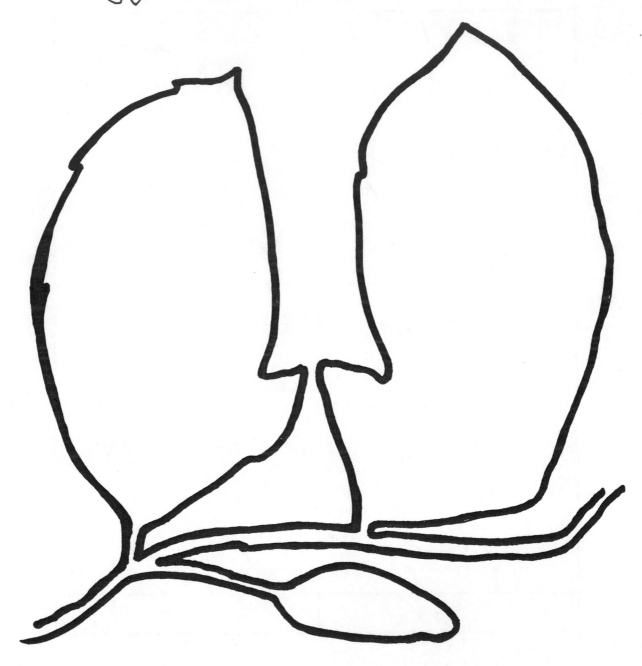

Early settlers made a bright yellow dye from sassafras bark. Indians liked to use it to spice their food. Sassafras tea was used as a medicine to help people when they had a cold.

Name _____

Date _____

RECIPE FOR MAKING PAPER

Materials needed: old newspapers, dishpan, water, one-half teaspoon liquid detergent, 3-by-3-inch piece of window screen, wooden spoon, sponge, paper towels, iron

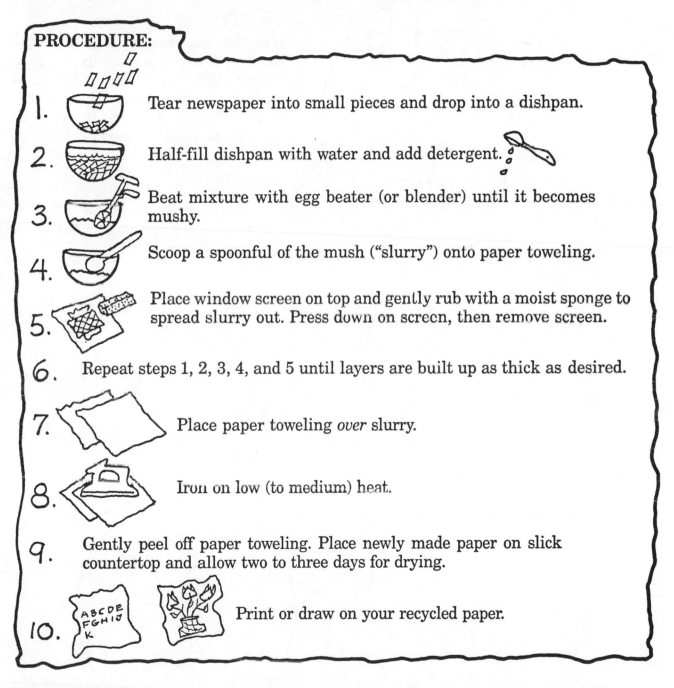

PROCEDURE:

1. Tear newspaper into small pieces and drop into a dishpan.

2. Half-fill dishpan with water and add detergent.

3. Beat mixture with egg beater (or blender) until it becomes mushy.

4. Scoop a spoonful of the mush ("slurry") onto paper toweling.

5. Place window screen on top and gently rub with a moist sponge to spread slurry out. Press down on screen, then remove screen.

6. Repeat steps 1, 2, 3, 4, and 5 until layers are built up as thick as desired.

7. Place paper toweling *over* slurry.

8. Iron on low (to medium) heat.

9. Gently peel off paper toweling. Place newly made paper on slick countertop and allow two to three days for drying.

10. Print or draw on your recycled paper.

NOTE: Keep this recipe handy and use it with your family. Increase the size of the screen to make larger pieces. Use for invitations, special announcements, or for artwork (draw on it with felt pen).

Name _____

Date _____

TAKING A CLOSER LOOK AT TREES

A botanist is a person who studies plants. A microscope is a tool used for observing small detail.

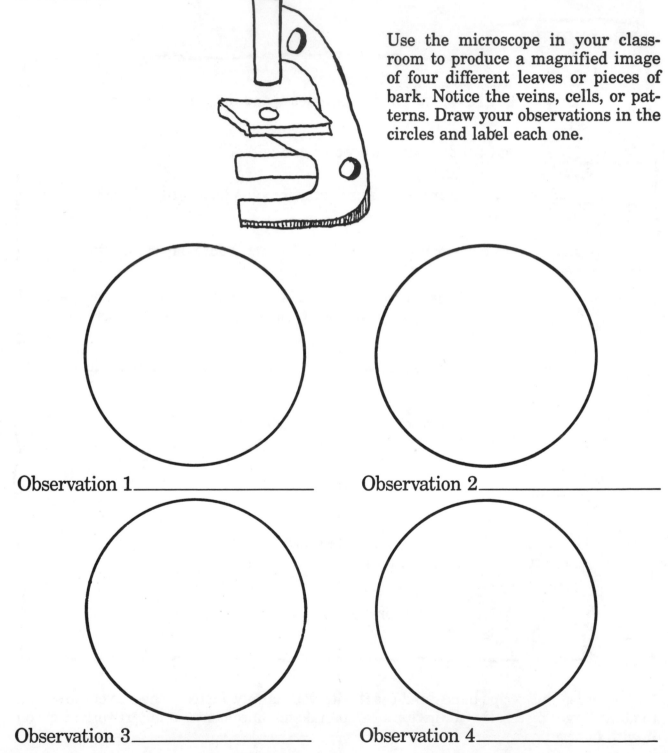

Use the microscope in your classroom to produce a magnified image of four different leaves or pieces of bark. Notice the veins, cells, or patterns. Draw your observations in the circles and label each one.

Observation 1 _____

Observation 2 _____

Observation 3 _____

Observation 4 _____

Name _____

Date _____

AUTUMN LEAVES ARE FALLING

Use the following A, B, C formula to complete the equations:

A. How many leaves are there all together in the picture? Put that number in Square A.

B. How many leaves fell to the ground? Put that number in Square B.

C. How many leaves are left on the tree? Put that number in Square C.

Example:

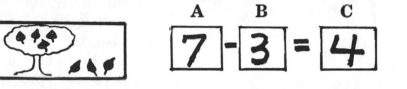

Name _____

Date _____

THE HIDDEN HALF

Roots are the hidden part of the tree. They can grow for miles to seek water and help nourish the tree. Roots also keep the soil from eroding.

Find the hidden half of each picture below and draw a line to it. What does the picture become? (HINT: Half of the pictures are fruits that grow on trees and the other half are paper byproducts of trees.)

Name _____

Date _____

TREE TALK

This tree is 300 feet tall and about 4,000 years old! Notice that a road has been built right through it. This tree has seen and heard a lot!

Pretend you could call the tree on the telephone and talk with it. List at least ten things the tree could talk about.

1. _____
2. _____
3. _____
4. _____
5. _____
6. _____
7. _____
8. _____
9. _____
10. _____

Name _____

Date _____

MATCH THE LEAF SHAPES

Color the two leaves in each row that are the same. Put an X on the one that is different.

Name _____

Date _____

AN ACORN STORY

Finish this story from the point of view of an acorn. Try to make it an exciting adventure! Use the back of this sheet if you need more space to write.

TITLE _____

Oh it's a beautiful day! I wish I could get started on my way to becoming a wonderful oak tree. SHHH! I hear something. It's a funny animal with a huge, bushy tail and it's coming right this way.

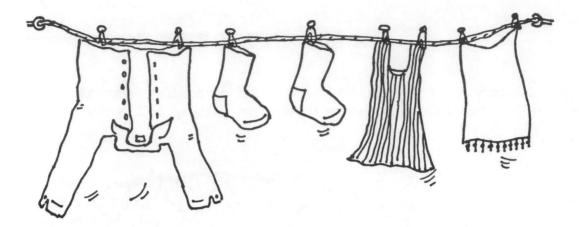

Section 15
THE WAYS OF THE WIND

Background Ideas and Other
Helpful Things to Know

The wind is air that moves from one place to another. Wind may blow so softly and gently that it can hardly be felt; other times, it can blow so fast and hard that it damages buildings and knocks down trees. Strong winds can churn up the ocean waves and damage ships or flood the land along the coast. Wind can blow clothing on a clothesline dry. It can push the blades of a windmill so that energy or electricity is created. Wind helps children fly kites and sailors float across the water in sailboats. Wind can be both helpful and harmful.

Wind is caused by uneven heating of the air around the earth by the sun. Two features of wind—its speed and its direction—are used in describing and forecasting weather. Wind speed is measured with an instrument called an "anemometer." Wind direction is measured with an instrument called a "weather vane."

Wind is a natural force, but wind can be made by people, too. Fans and air conditioners are examples of man-made wind. Using our mouths to blow also makes wind when we blow bubbles or whistles or musical instruments or the candles on a birthday cake.

Activity Suggestions

Language Experience Chart. Gather the students together and have them dictate a language experience story about the wind. You might write about "How do we know if it's a windy day?" or "Things to do on a windy day." The children can copy the story onto their own sheets of paper and draw a picture that illustrates the words.

Colored Bubbles. Everyone enjoys blowing bubbles! Pick a sunny day to go outside for this adventure. Give each child a small margarine tub or a paper cup about one-third full of soap bubble solution and a plastic straw to blow bubbles. Here is a recipe for homemade bubbles:

  1 cup granulated soap or soap powder
  1 quart warm water
  liquid food coloring
  small margerine tub or paper cup for each child
  plastic straw for each child

Dissolve the soap in the warm water. Then stir in the food coloring, mix, and pour into the individual cups. Remind the children that they should suck just a little bit of the soap mixture into the straw and then blow it out. They won't want to get the soap mixture in their mouths! Often the bubble mixture will stay on the bottom of the straw when dipped into the cup.

Seeds Blown by the Wind. The wind is responsible for blowing the seeds from plants and trees and spreading them to places where new plants will then grow. Talk about the kinds of seeds that the wind may spread and ask the children if they have any plants growing in their yards that were not planted there. Have them draw pictures of the plants or bring in samples to share with the rest of the class.

Making Pinwheels. Pinwheels are fun to make. Cut squares of very thin paper. Cut in from each corner to the center of the square, being careful not to have the cuts meet. Fold over alternate corners and push a straight pin through the corners and into a plastic straw. Place a small lump of clay over the pointed end of the pin for protection. Let the students take these pinwheels outdoors on a sunny, breezy day.

Paper Airplanes. Teach the children to make paper airplanes by folding sheets of paper and decorating them with markers or crayons. Take the airplanes outside on a windy day. Have the students stand behind a designated line and throw their planes. When the airplanes have landed, encourage the children to use measuring wheels to see how far their planes have traveled.

The Dangers of Wind. Heavy winds of severe storms or tornadoes can be very damaging. Talk with students about why tornadoes form and their potential danger. Go over your school's rules, if any, for tornado drills, and practice the procedures so that everyone feels safe and comfortable.

Homemade Kites. Cut out paper kites from construction paper and have the students decorate them with pieces of brightly colored paper glued in place. Make a tail and ties out of scraps of material or strips of crepe paper, and attach a string to the kite. Tell the children that when they hold onto the string and run, the kite will fly out behind them.

Activity Sheets for
THE WAYS OF THE WIND

Name _____

Date _____

WINDY WASHDAY WORDS

The wind is drying these clothes on the line. Moving from left to right, do the following: Color the third item of clothing red. Color the fifth item of clothing yellow. Color the first item of clothing blue. Color the fourth item of clothing red. Color the second item of clothing orange.

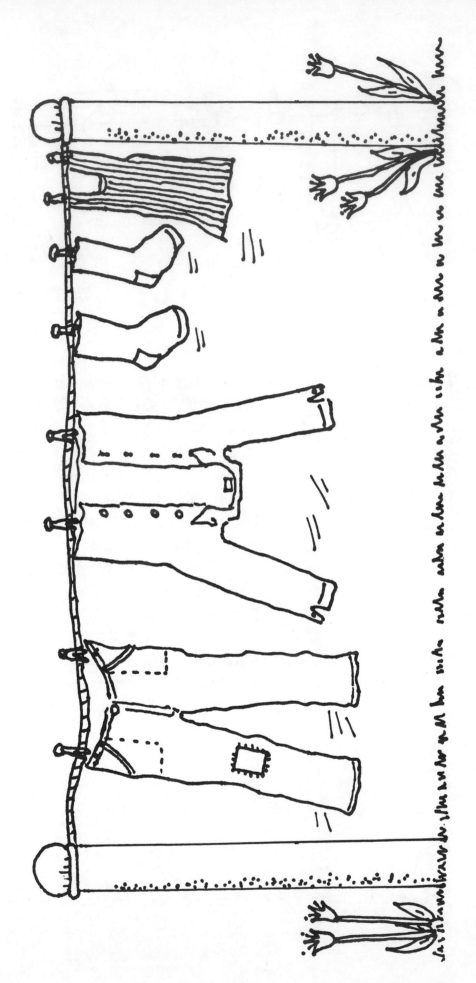

Name _____

Date _____

UP, UP, AND AWAY
IN A HOT AIR BALLOON

Write a story about a trip in a hot air balloon. The wind will help you move. Use the back of this sheet if you need more space to write.

Where will we go today?

Name _____

Date _____

HIGH FLYING NUMBERS

The wind is great for flying kites! Draw a line to match the number sentence on the left to the kite with the correct answer on the right. When you're finished, color the kites.

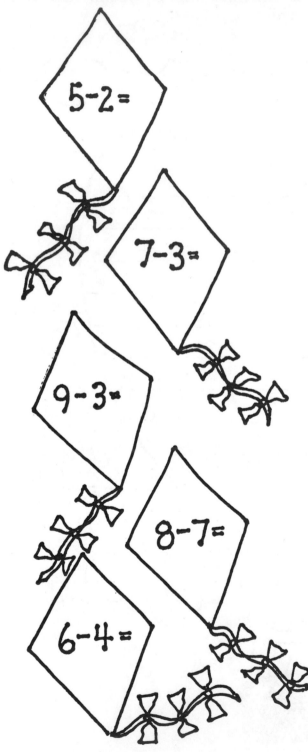

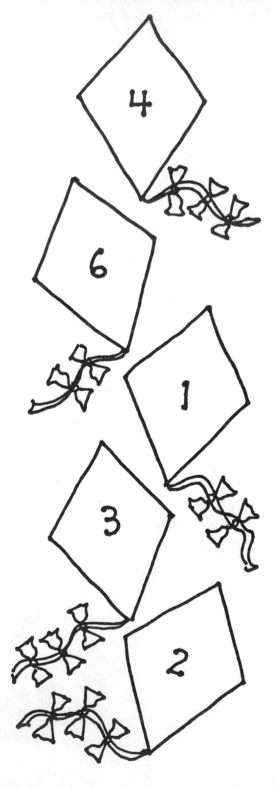

Name

Date

CATCH THE NUMBER WORD TRASH

The wind is scattering paper trash from this garbage can all over the place! You can help clean it up by writing the correct numeral on each paper scrap.

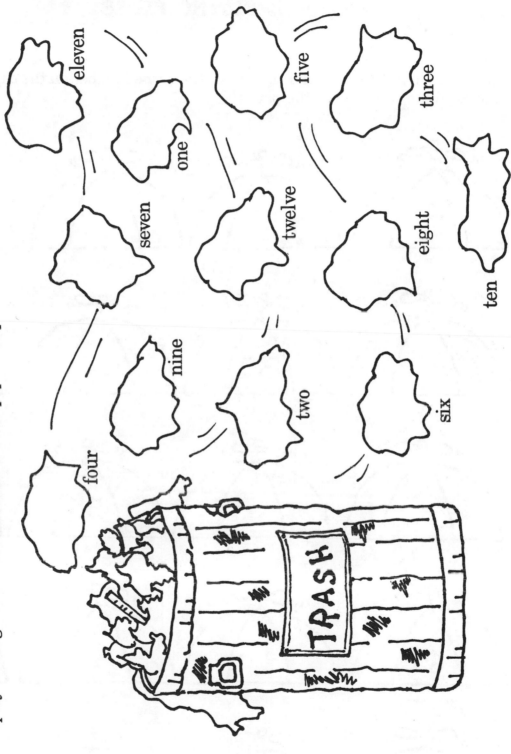

Name _____

Date _____

FLYING FIVES

The wind can blow the propellers on these caps if you can count by fives. If the number on the cap ends in zero, color the cap yellow. If the number on the cap ends in five, color the cap blue. Do you see the pattern?

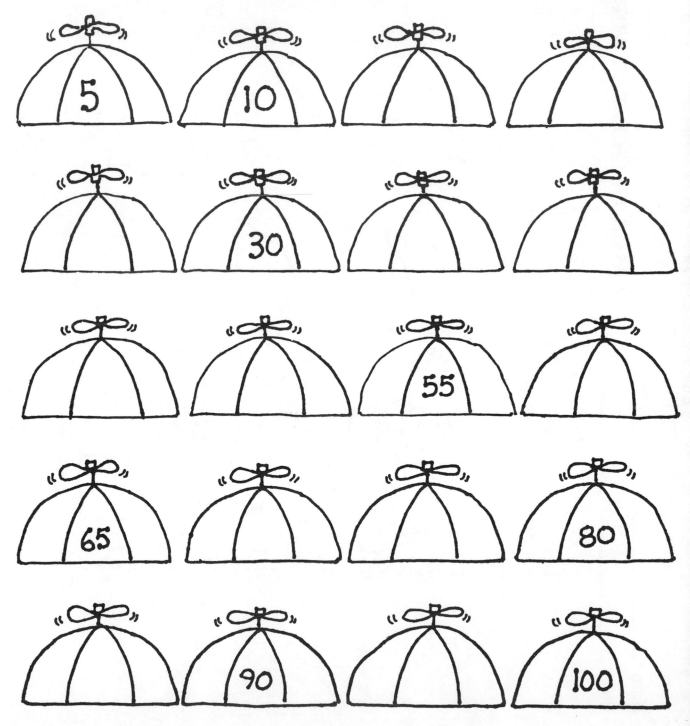

Name _____

Date _____

BUBBLE LETTERS

The wind is blowing these bubbles away. Before they disappear, print the correct lower-case letter next to the capital letter in each bubble. When you're finished, color the bottle and the bubbles.

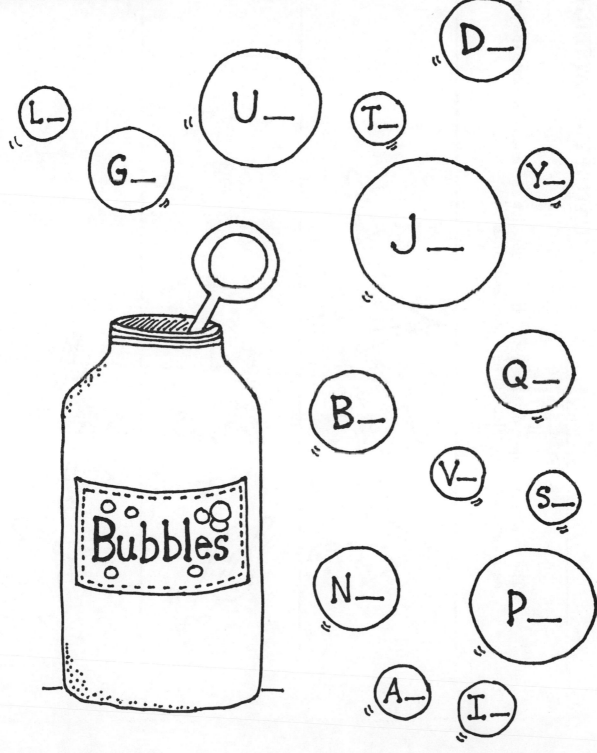

Name _____

Date _____

CATCH THE PATTERN

The wind has made a pattern out of these umbrellas and hats. Complete the pattern in each row and then color the hats and umbrellas.

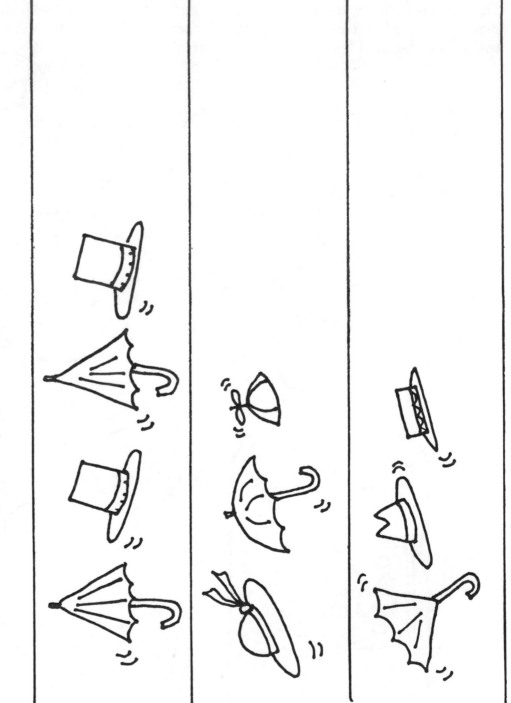

Name _____

Date _____

FAVORITE FAN GRAPH

Some wind is made by people, not nature. Ask twelve of your friends to pick their favorite kind of people- (or dog-) made wind. Each person should write his or her name in the box below his or her choice, starting with the top box in each column. Which kind of wind was the most favorite? Which was the least favorite? Were there any equal votes?

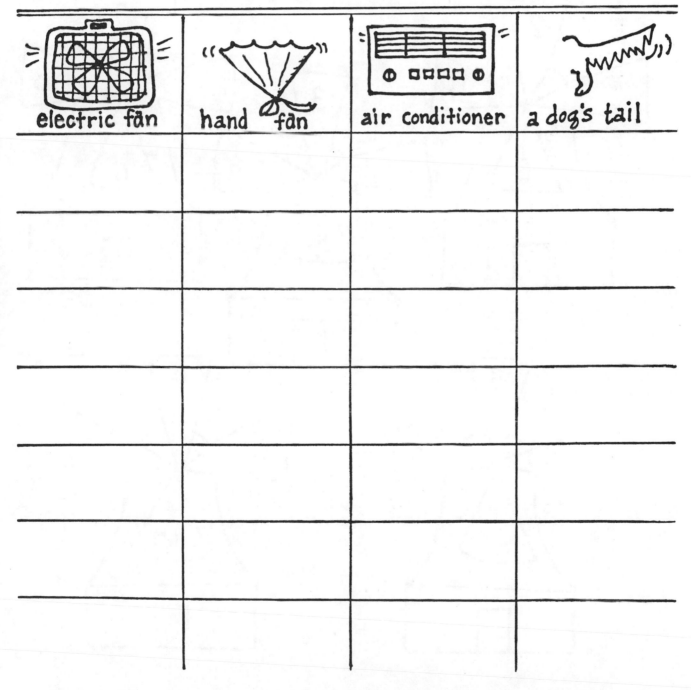

electric fan	hand fan	air conditioner	a dog's tail

Name _____

Date _____

WINDMILL NUMBERS

The wind turns windmill blades to help create energy or electricity. Each windmill below has a series of numbers on the blades that are a special pattern. Try to figure out each pattern. Then write the missing number of the pattern on the empty blade.

Name _____

Date _____

SAILING WITH THE WIND

Sailboats move across the water by the power of the wind blowing into their sails. Color these sailboats. Then cut them out and place them in order from smallest to largest.

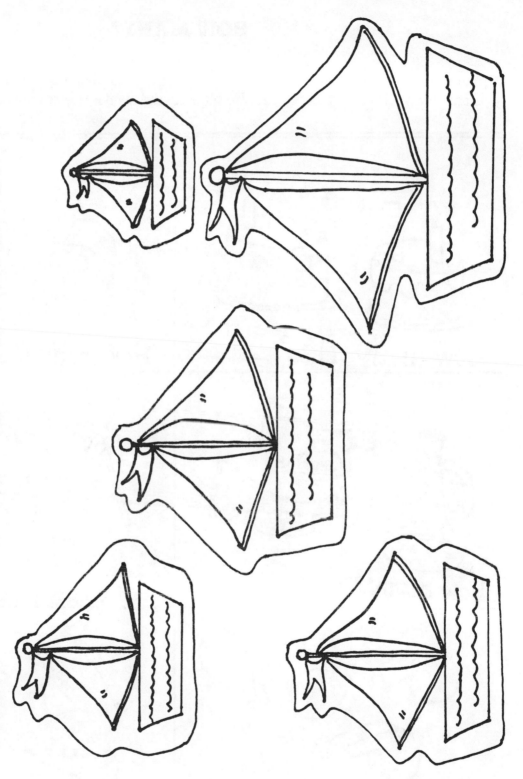

Name _____

Date _____

HOW MANY?

You can make wind with your mouth by blowing. All of the objects below are things that you can blow. In each box, count the objects and write the correct answer on the line.

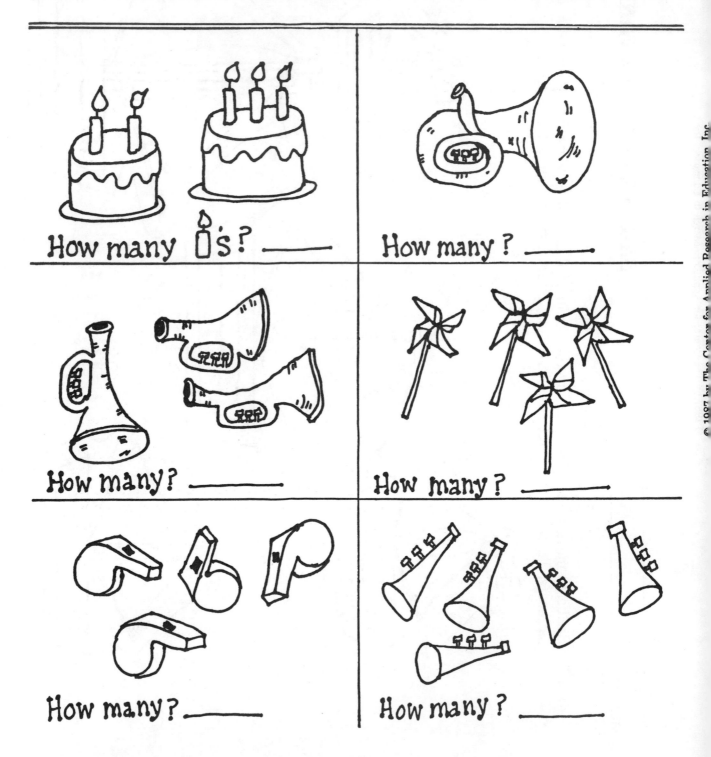

How many 🕯's? _____

How many ? _____

How many? _____

How many ? _____

How many? _____

How many ? _____

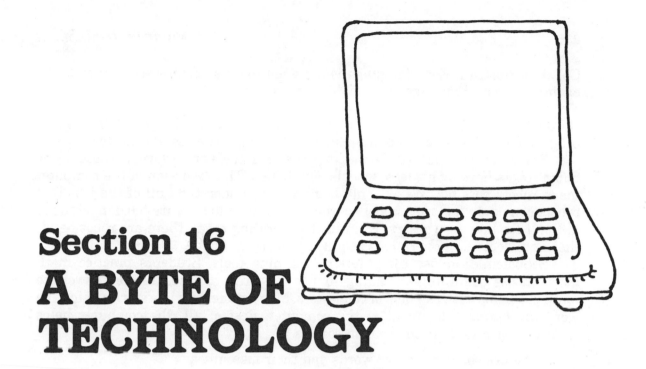

Section 16
A BYTE OF TECHNOLOGY

Background Ideas and Other Helpful Things to Know

Computers are tools that help people remember enormous amounts of information for as long as it is needed. A computer can do only what the person running it (called the programmor) tells it to do. This machine cannot feel happy or sad or think its own ideas. It really cannot even combine thoughts the way our brains can. It can, however, do some of the jobs that our brains can and complete them more quickly than we can. A computer can obey a list of commands stored in its memory. The programmer can give the computer these commands by typing them on an electric typewriter wired to the computer.

What can computers do? They are good at figuring out arithmetic problems, making decisions, and controlling other machines such as robots, spaceships, weather forecasting equipment, traffic lights, and telephone equipment. Computers can play video games and make music. Some of them can even talk in strange voices. Remember, though, that these talking machines can say only what the programmer directs them to say.

What can't computers do? They can't think their own thoughts or decide what they want to remember and what they want to forget. They can't cry or laugh or hug. They can't see or hear or touch or smell—at least, not yet! But scientists are teaching them to do many things.

Computers are programmed to understand special languages. Just as some people speak French, Spanish or Italian, some computers know Basic, Logo,

Cobol, or Fortran. Each language is designed to do a certain activity best. For example, Basic language is used to perform numerical tasks and to produce pictures. Logo is a problem-solving language that can be used even by very young children. It is capable of drawing pictures and of working with words and lists. A programmer must know the language needed to get the results wanted.

Robots are computerized machines that can move or perform specific tasks. Some robots have arms, legs, wheels, and hands. The invention of the computer made robots possible. We are only beginning to understand all of the jobs that robots can do. In factories, robots perform assignments that are too dangerous or difficult for human workers. Even in the operating room, there are robot hands that help doctors in operations requiring precise skills.

Schoolchildren use computers as learning tools. Students practice math facts, choose beginning or ending sounds in words, and decide the answers to math problems with the help of computers. Many students write stories using the word processing component of the computer. Best of all, the computer helps children learn to be good problem solvers.

Here are some computer words and their meanings:

bug: a mistake in the computer program

byte: a measure of the amount of information that a computer can process and store

calculator: a machine that is controlled by a computer chip; it helps us with numbers but doesn't have much memory

chip: a silicon plate with many transistors that makes up a memory circuit; it is located inside the computer

circuit: many transistors working together

computer: a machine that can store large amounts of information and perform many tasks

program: a list of orders or commands that are written in computer language and given to the computer

transistor: the simplest computer pathway that carries information

Activity Suggestions

Field Trip. Take a field trip to a computer store or visit a firm that uses computers in its work. Talk about the capabilities of the computers and how jobs would be different without them.

Class Visitors. Ask a person who works with computers to come to class and talk about his or her job and other jobs that are available in the computer field. Ask the visitor about the training needed and the prospects for those with technical training in the future.

Ask the school superintendent or treasurer to visit your classroom and talk about what your school district is doing to incorporate computers into both business and instructional aspects of the educational program.

Design a Robot. Discuss the jobs that robots can do. Have each student design a robot and write an accompanying story about the special features of the robot, what needs to be done to keep it in working order, and what extraordinary jobs the robot can perform.

Have the children bring in cardboard boxes, paper rolls, small pieces of wood, bottle caps, dowel rods, and other materials. Encourage each child to fashion a robot from the assortment of items and then paint it or color it with markers.

"A-maze" Classmates. Have the children create their own mazes and exchange them with other classmates to see if they can be solved.

A Byte Breakfast. In celebration of the computer, have a byte breakfast. The food served at the breakfast should all be byte-sized, such as donut holes; chunks of peaches, oranges, and pineapple mixed together with coconut and cherries; tiny biscuits with dabs of butter and honey; granola bars cut into bite-sized pieces; and small cups of juice.

Delicious Chips. Since we talk about the chips of a computer, make a list of other kinds of chips: potato chips, banana chips, sesame chips, coconut chips, chocolate chips, butterscotch chips, and so on. Have a tasting party with various kinds of chips. Here's one recipe for chocolate chip cookies that the students can help you make:

1 cup shortening

¾ cup brown sugar, firmly packed

¾ cup white sugar

2 eggs

1 tablespoon hot water

1 teaspoon vanilla

1½ cups sifted flour

1 teaspoon soda

1 teaspoon salt

2 cups quick oatmeal

2 cups chocolate chips

Sift the flour with the soda and salt. Cream the shortening and sugar together and add the eggs one at a time. Add hot water to the creamed mixture. Then add the dry ingredients. Use a teaspoon to drop the dough onto a cookie sheet and bake at 375°F for 8 to 11 minutes.

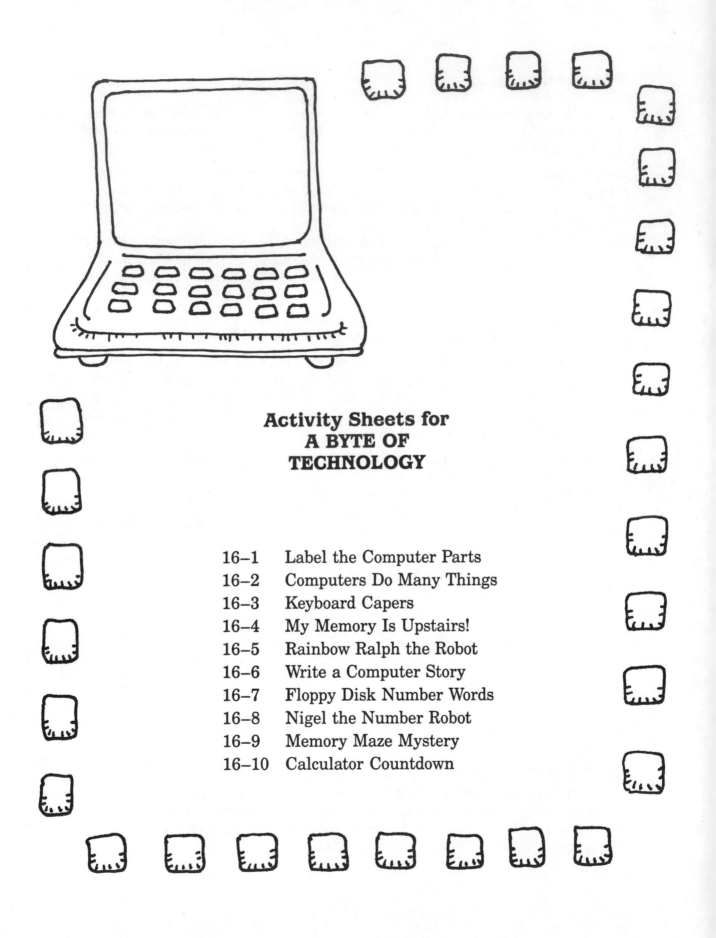

Activity Sheets for
A BYTE OF
TECHNOLOGY

Name

Date

LABEL THE COMPUTER PARTS

Cut out the words at the bottom of the page and paste each one next to the correct computer part.

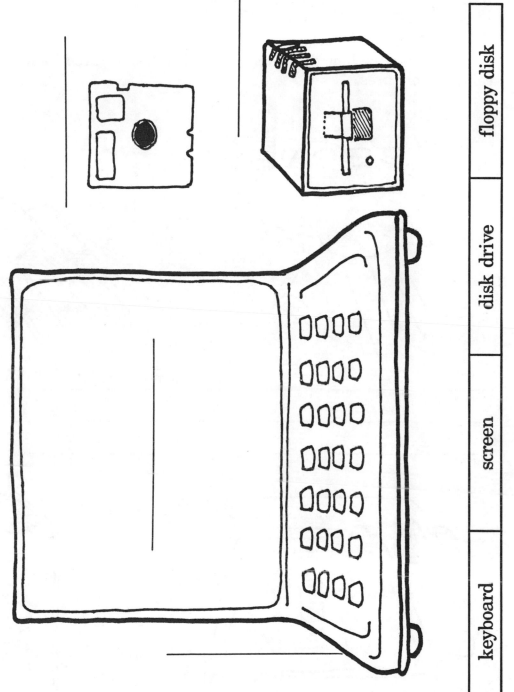

| keyboard | screen | disk drive | floppy disk |

Name _____

Date _____

COMPUTERS DO MANY THINGS

Computers help us perform many jobs. On the lines below each picture, write a few words to describe how computers help with that pictured item. When you're finished, color the pictures.

_____

_____

_____

_____

_____

_____

Name _____

Date _____

KEYBOARD CAPERS

Study the picture of the computer keyboard here. Can you type your name on the keyboard? Can you type the name of your school? Can you type the name of your town? Can you type your age? Can you type your spelling words? Don't forget to use the space bar! Now use an orange crayon to color the letters that spell your name. Use a yellow crayon to color the number that tells your age.

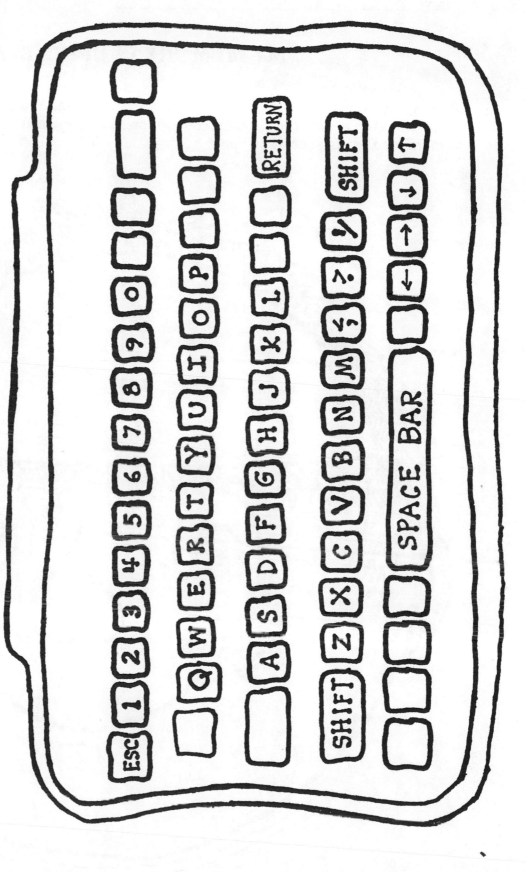

Name _____

Date _____

MY MEMORY IS UPSTAIRS!

A computer has a memory where it stores information. You have a memory, too, where your thoughts are stored. In each compartment below, draw a picture of something you remember that is special to you.

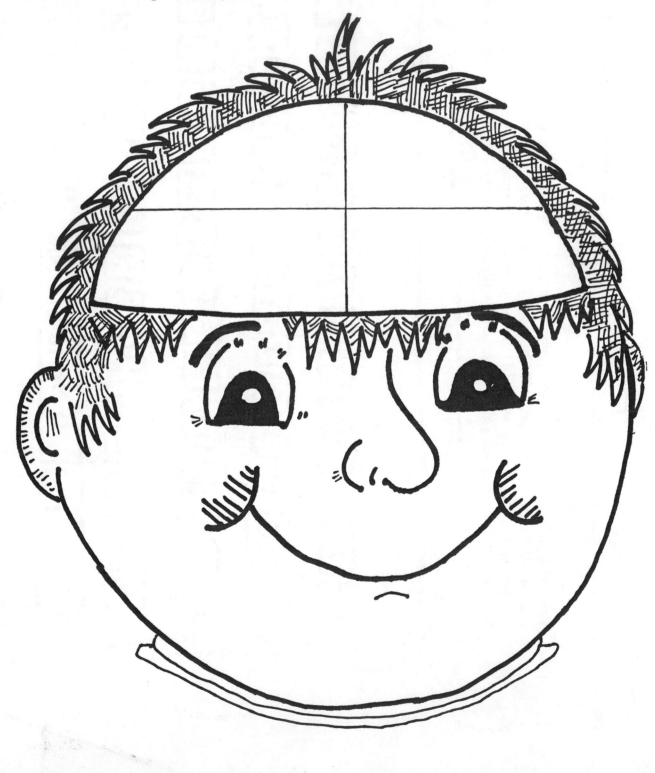

Name _____

Date _____

RAINBOW RALPH THE ROBOT

Robots are machines with computer brains. They can move or perform special tasks. Color "Rainbow Ralph" using this code: 1—orange; 2—red; 3—yellow; 4—green; 5—blue; 6—purple.

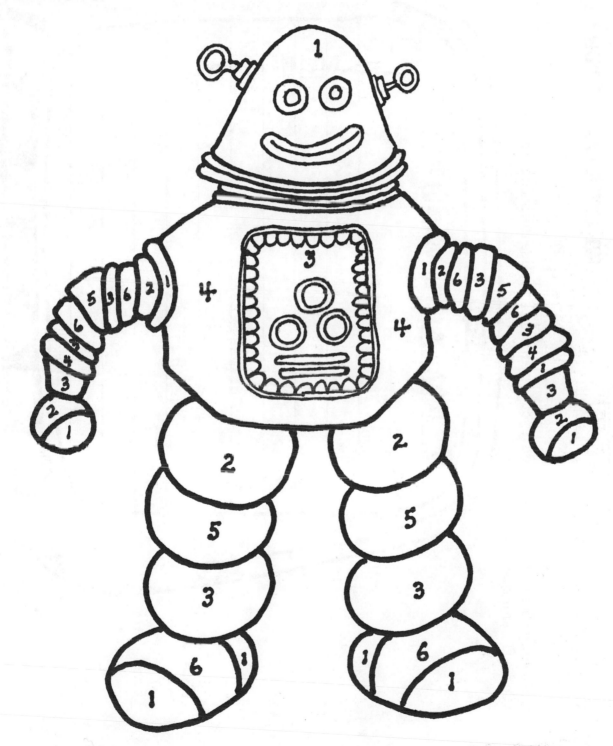

WRITE A COMPUTER STORY

Name _____

Date _____

Write a story about what you would do if you were a computer. Use the back of this sheet if you need more space to write.

I AM A COMPUTER...

Name _____

Date _____

FLOPPY DISK NUMBER WORDS

Read the number under each floppy disk and write the correct matching numeral on each disk label. The first one has been done for you. When you're finished, color the odd-numbered disks in light colors and the even-numbered disks in dark colors.

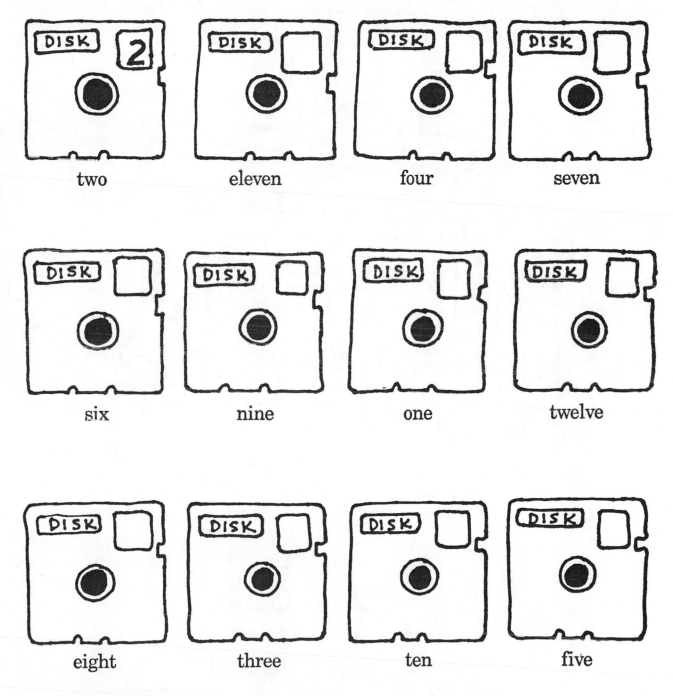

two   eleven   four   seven

six   nine   one   twelve

eight   three   ten   five

Name _____

Date _____

NIGEL THE NUMBER ROBOT

Nigel the Number Robot is ready to go to work as soon as all of his numbers are in place. Write the missing numbers in the boxes so that Nigel can start moving. When you're finished, color Nigel.

Name _____

Date _____

MEMORY MAZE MYSTERY

The inside of a computer is made up of little wires, pathways, and tunnels that carry information. The pathways and tunnels are so small that you would need a microscope to see them. The simplest pathways are called "transistors." See if you can find a pathway through this memory maze so that the message gets to the receiver. Color the pathway red. Be careful!

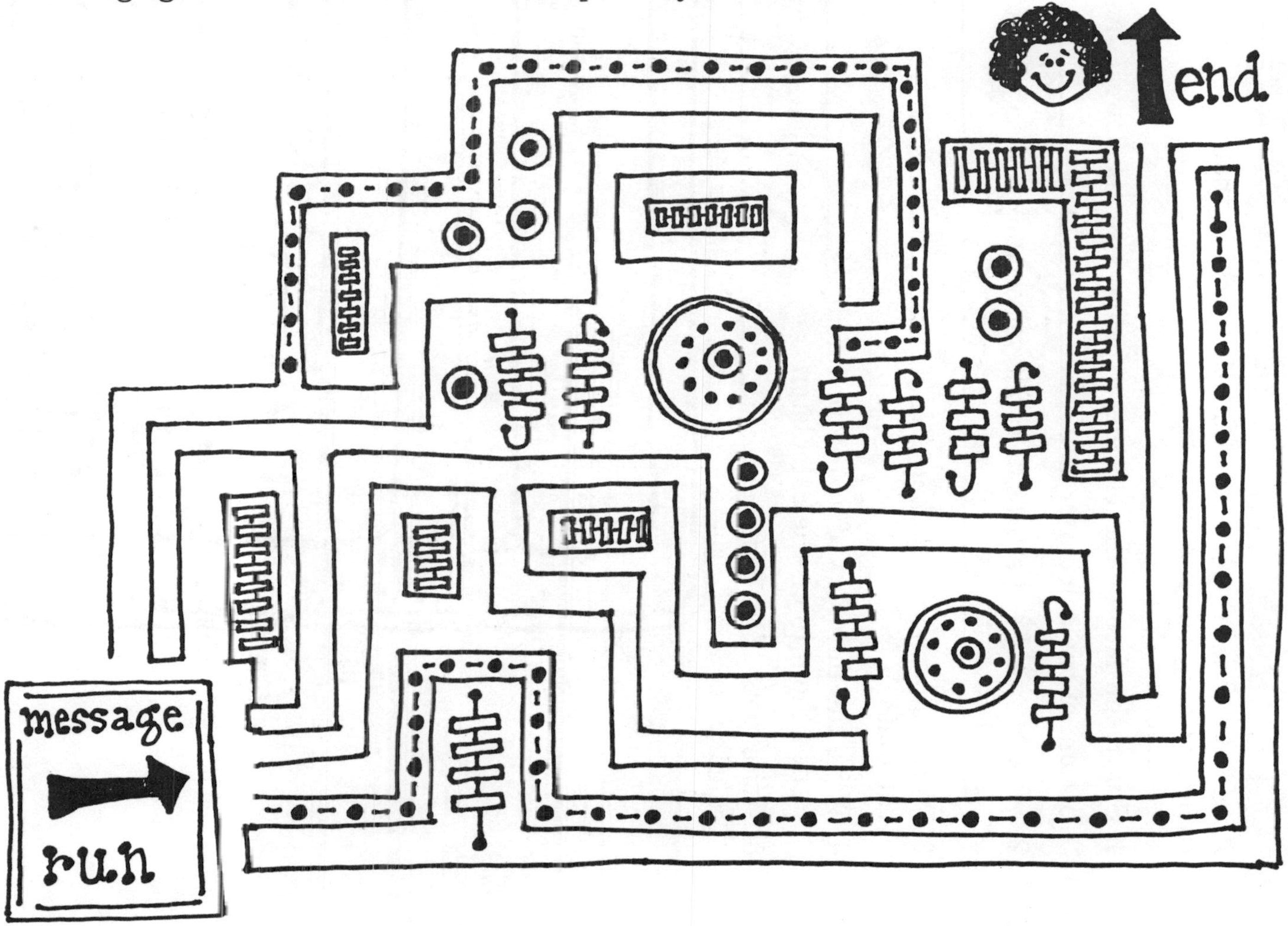

Name _____

Date _____

CALCULATOR COUNTDOWN

A calculator is a special arithmetic machine that helps us with numbers. It has a computer chip but not much memory.

1. Study the face of the calculator below. Are the lowest numbers at the top or the bottom of the calculator? _____

2. What would be the first key that you would need to push to use the calculator?

_____

3. Write your phone number. _____ Punch it in on the calculator.

4. Write the numbers of your street address. _____
   Punch them in on the calculator.

5. Write your ZIP code. _____ Punch it in on the calculator.